THE
SELF
VOWS

THE
SELF
VOWS

Seven Vows that will change your life

Dr. Michelle R. Hannah

THE SELF VOWS
SEVEN VOWS THAT WILL CHANGE YOUR LIFE

iUniverse books may be ordered through booksellers or by contacting:

iUniverse
1663 Liberty Drive
Bloomington, IN 47403
www.iuniverse.com
1-800-Authors (1-800-288-4677)

ISBN: 978-1-5320-9446-0 (sc)
ISBN: 978-1-5320-9447-7 (e)

Library of Congress Control Number: 2020902477

Print information available on the last page.

iUniverse rev. date: 05/22/2020

To all women I have coached and to those I have never
met, I give you the gift of *The Self Vows.*
I would like to extend a special dedication to every woman and man who took
a chance and trusted in the process of the Self Vows program. I love you!

CONTENTS

FOREWORD

I am an advanced certified colon hydrotherapist, instructor, and GPACT co–vice president. I have been a colon therapist for thirteen years. I have many certifications, and I am a certified instructor in massage, yoga, and Pilates.

My profession requires me to be able to relate to the public on a very compassionate level. To be of the highest service to my clients, I had to go within myself. I had to live the lifestyle of a cleansing professional. One thing I know about the body is that when you cleanse the internal atmosphere, it includes the emotional and spiritual beliefs that you hold true and dear. That being said, I noticed that behaviors from before I started cleansing began to disappear, and for the good. My relating to others improved, and my relationship with myself shifted greatly.

I speak from truth and experience and with an open heart to educate my clients before they even schedule an appointment with me. My goal is to awaken the educator-healer within each client, and doing so goes way beyond selling a service or product. I have to lead by example and be able to explain what I do on a very simple level. In order to do that, I have to love what I do and believe in my ability to do so.

In April 2018, I was able to purchase ten acres of land for my fortieth birthday. This year, for my forty-first birthday I purchased twenty additional acres and a home across the street from my first purchase with the goal of hosting a monthly Off-Grid Healing Retreat for Women of Color. I am the first woman in my family not only to own and operate a business completely on my own but also to host retreats on property that I own. Moving through this process has taught me that staying focused regardless of appearances and moving through it even when I am tired and have zero dollars in my account is very much worth it. I cannot explain enough how staying committed to the vows I created for myself held that sacred space for me to keep going.

I have been engaged two times, both—if I remember correctly—out of obligation or duty because at the time everyone was getting married. It was the thing to do during that period in my life. However, with both engagements I never made it to saying I do.

In hindsight, I knew deep down that I was not ready to be a wife to a man who barely knew himself. And, truth be told, I very much did not know who I was or what I wanted to do, much less get married. Many of my friends recommended I do it anyway, saying he was a nice guy and we made a cute couple, but I knew marriage was more than those statements. Those same friends are now divorced, some twice.

The business of relating, for most people, does not become clear or understood until adulthood. Relating, or lack thereof, is a part of being that I see all too often in my business as a colon therapist. It shows up in my clients as constipation, confusion, and sometimes anger. Dr. Michelle R. Hannah and I often discuss that how we do one thing is how we do everything, including relating and relationships, until we break the cycle and start to live as our most authentic selves. But what does that look like? How does one get to that point? We regularly discuss what emotional constipation looks like, the importance of asking for what you need and want, as well as how self-care plays a huge role in successful relationships with others and the need to create healthy boundaries to maintain a level of inner peace. Ah … as two friends sit and talk about relationships, it all becomes clear.

Michelle has this beautiful way of guiding both men and women through the intricacies of our most inner desires to create this beautiful composition called love. On occasion, our dialogues have left me speechless because they have been that powerful and have moved me to act. Through our conversations, Michelle has opened my eyes to the fact that I can have a passion-filled and supportive relationship and a thriving business without sacrificing my basic needs.

Now in my forties, as I look back at my history of dating men and dialoging with Michelle, I have realized a couple of strong points about relationships:

- Relationships are mirrors of the deepest truth about self.
- Eventually, truth will always rise to the surface.
- There is no rush in understanding what I need, want, or desire.
- My emotions and feelings are valid, accurate, and true for me.
- I am the only one who can validate or approve my position within a relationship.
- Ultimately, the experience of being in a relationship is mine to create.

This book propels you to get clear about going "there," which is diving deep into those parts that we neatly tuck away. However, it is only a matter of time before all that stuff you put to the side comes busting out of the seams and spilling over into your life. This book challenges you to ask yourself, When a woman is asked to become a wife, what does that really mean? When a man decides that he is ready to provide as a husband, what does that shift look like for him? These are questions I continue to ask myself on a deeper level, because what I know for sure is that there is nothing higher on the planet than a man and woman who have made the commitment to ride this wave of life together. Balance is the key to living an amazing life, and we are created to become that perfect balance together. However, the fulfillment of this right does not come from the other person; it comes from you. Michelle has created the perfect clarity and foundation to get you to this vulnerable yet powerful position.

As you can see, creating a loving and supportive connection between a man and a woman starts with loving and supporting yourself, creating healthy boundaries, and becoming clear about what works for you and what does not. Doing so has not only helped me to work through my relationship woes, but it has also allowed me to transfer the same energy into my business and relate to other men in my life, such as my son, my family members, and my clients. Working through my past experiences has helped me see the baggage I was dragging from previous relationships into my current ones, and it gave me the tools to break up the negative so that a positive shift could happen. These are the points of Michelle's books, looking at our not-so-pleasant stuff so that the same energy is not dragged into our relationships and does not become the foundation upon which future relationships are built.

Michelle's consistency and drive to be present with couples and singles creates the perfect environment to go deep and unearth the gunk that we often get stuck in. This is where the work happens, this is where the shift happens, and this is where the simplicity and practice of caring for your heart space is learned. If this step is overlooked, creating and being part of a loving relationship may not evolve in the way you would like, and the foundation you thought you had may crumble.

Michelle has thought this whole piece out. She has been there, sat in her frustration and understanding about her relationships, and done the work. The key phrase here is *the work*. Thus, she created the Self Vows program. This first book takes you on an emotional, spiritual, and physical trip of accountability on how you are participating in love, life, and commitment to self. What I know for sure is that we have all the answers to our questions; it only requires that we get still and listen. Michelle's book guides you in doing just that. It requires you to go within, dig deep, feel the stuff you've tucked away, unpack it, look at it, and see it. It challenges you to have the tough conversations with yourself before you ever consider having them with another. The truth is my clients need to take the self vows along with taking care of their physical health. It is all connected.

Begin this journey with an open heart and open mind. Love yourself *first* throughout this entire process. If you need to pause, pause. If you need to talk, reach out to someone. Breathe through this and trust that you have everything you need to be happy and to be in a relationship that reflects this. Embrace this book, embrace your healing, embrace everything about where you are at the present moment, and embrace the lessons and tough conversations that this book will challenge you to have. Most of all, embrace the love that comes from the personal stories, me, and Dr. Michelle R. Hannah. She is giving you this amazing gift, *The Self Vows: Seven Vows That Will Change Your Life.* Enjoy!

Monisha Denise Garner

PREFACE

After working twenty years in corporate America in the capacity of an assistant dean, a coach and trainer for personal development, a manager of strategic partnerships, a public speaker, and a master relationship coach, I have found that the common denominator among all people is the need to understand and connect more deeply in our relationships. Whether it's conflict resolution, team collaboration, personal or behavioral development, CEO or CFO challenges with time management, or fear of speaking to an audience, at the foundation of every problem are people's struggles in their personal relationships and their lack of tools to connect to others. With that said, I realized that I not only had a unique way of introducing and navigating people through tough conversations, but I was also able to connect people back to themselves and significant others back to each other.

The baby that I've been waiting to birth is the Self Vows program, which was ushered into existence after many couples started to enroll in my original program, the Vows. I developed the Self Vows program in 2018. The program answers many questions about the relationship with self and provides many options for how to uncover the truth, how to live authentically, and, ultimately, how to fall in love with yourself no matter the challenges. In case you're not familiar with the Vows program, allow me to introduce you. It is a ten-week program that takes couples through traditional wedding vows in a unique and intimate way. I started the Vows program specifically for couples to work through together. It took me months to tweak the questions, tips, and exercises. My clients were instrumental in assisting me with identifying and perfecting the questions that had the greatest impact, deepened their connections, and ultimately freed them to be honest with one another so that they could live happy and fulfilled lives.

The Vows program challenges members of a couple to question whether they truly support and accept themselves where they are so that they can accept their mates where they are and know how to support the people they say they love. They face the tough conversations about finances; after all, they are vowing "for richer, for poorer." Couples figure out what "for better, for worse" means for their relationships and truly come to understand what it means to love and cherish. Couples find that the "in sickness and in health" segment truly challenges them to answer very tough questions, and they realize that they're making this commitment until they take their last breaths. Couples who complete the program with the intention to heal, deeply reflect, love harder every day, and evolve consistently have transformational results. Their relationships are never the same, for the better.

After many couples completed the program, I began to dig deeper with the questions and realized I needed to separate the members of each couple and ask them similar questions but from a single's perspective. The result was amazing. The program started to form. They started to uncover the dishonesty and lack of trust with themselves, and they realized how this affected their relationships. They began to understand the concept of transparency and the importance of vulnerability.

After coaching many couples and writing *The Vows* book, I began to realize people needed to strongly consider taking the traditional wedding vows to the self first. *The Vows* is the blueprint for how to effectively commit to the traditional wedding vows daily within your marriage.

Funnily, most people can't even remember the vows, let alone commit and exercise them daily. The book ushered them into having the tough conversations about finance, passion, intimacy, love, heath, commitment, grief, and living with intention. It asks more than two hundred reflective questions while keeping readers engaged with personal stories, tips, and interactive exercises. Couples who take the Vows program have decided to get married or not be married and to begin a great friendship instead. Couples have unleashed a new passion, or their relationships have been reinvented through the Vows process. I realized in sessions that if we made the decision to take those vows to the self, we would show up differently in our relationships. We would be able to share our love in a healthier way.

Once I started to teach this, clients were so fascinated and connected to what I was teaching that they needed their own sessions because there was so much hidden under the surface. Most clients realized that they were expecting their spouses to solve many issues for which they needed to take accountability. They needed some self-healing but expected their spouses to do it.

Because of the success of the Vows program and the book, I began to offer the self vows to my single clients. From there, it turned into a ten-week program that delves into the meaning and benefits of the vows. The benefits were freedom from the fake self and the desire to marry the authentic self. My single clients learned to accept things about themselves and to go through the process of evolving. They gained patience with self and began to make healthier decisions because they learned to trust self and stand unapologetically in their truth. They were no longer scared of vulnerability and found themselves allergic to anything other than transparency.

I can't explain the emotion I felt after seeing individual after individual break through their fear and pain to love. I was over the moon that so many of my clients found healthy relationships, and some decided to move on to marriage. The wonderful thing about this program is that even if you can't do it face-to-face with me, the retreats are open for anyone anywhere to attend. I would love to have you and meet you. Until then, enjoy the book, which echoes my face-to-face sessions and stories from others who have taken the self vows, as well as some who didn't.

The success of those sessions actually provided me a great gift, and for those of you who know me, you know I'm a giver. Keep reading, because today I'm giving the gift to you. That gift challenged me to dig deeper through helping my clients work through their own pain and fears. It caused me to question my intentions and pause when needed. I began to observe that I was an expert of self-love but was failing at self-care. The more I fine-tuned the program, the more I evolved and the more I forgave myself for things I wasn't aware I was still blaming myself for. I realized that this program, and now book, was actually a gift for me first. I'm so happy that I get to now share it with all of you!

I challenge you to take the vows to self first. Once you have done that and you're thinking about getting married or in need of a tune-up in your relationship, please read *The Vows*.

You will likely have many enlightened moments that result in clarity, peace, hope, and love. My hope is that you fall deeply in love with self. Here are some beautiful testimonials of people who have taken the self vows.

> It's hard to put into words what Michelle has done for me. She helped me find my inner glow. I felt like one of those people in "the sunken place" in the movie *Get Out* when I first started seeing her. But after a lot of hard work and effort of coming in every week for what felt like forever, I found her. When I say her, I mean the authentic, unapologetic, and beautiful woman I now see in the mirror. Granted, there's still some polishing and work to do, but I have finally got myself back. I am no longer a shell of a girl but rather a woman of grit and strength, who, as Michelle so often says, knows her worth. Self-love never looked so beautiful. This is the result when you commit to taking the self vows. I realized I had to leave everything about myself and support myself through breaking away from

the things that don't serve me. I needed to move forward. Funny how we grow up wanting to take this vow with another but do not do it for ourselves. And that is what Michelle has done for me. She has inspired me to come into my own.

—Xochitel Franco

Michelle taught me to express my thoughts and feelings. Prior to our sessions I didn't know how to address my feelings, which caused challenging issues in my interpersonal relationships. She helped me get unstuck so that I could emotionally, mentally, and spiritually connect to myself. Once I was able to do that, I was able to trust myself and my decisions. When you trust yourself, you will then know who to trust. I would recommend Michelle's Self Vows program one thousand times for anyone who is looking to take the self vows. Although I'm married, by taking the self vows first, I show up differently in my marriage. The self vows taught me to unleash my voice.

—Janae Floyd

Divorce, unhealthy relationships, low self-esteem, lack of self-worth, and being a people pleaser led me to take my own self vow. I knew I had to break the pattern of generations before me that willingly and unwillingly participated in unhealthy relationships, specifically those with self.

I took the journey. I lived my program, was a student, and continue to be a student. I never tell my clients to do exercises or ask and answer the tough questions if I haven't done them or practiced them daily. Taking the self vows first not only made it easier to overcome the challenges in my marriage and communicating with my partner, but it also helped me have healthier relationships in general.

I started this journey many moons ago, but I truly have realized that it's a journey and not a destination. I took my self vows, and I committed. However, I have realized that the more I grow, test, and challenge my commitment and execution of the vows, the more I flourish, and the vows take on a deeper meaning and sometimes a totally different perspective.

Once reconnected, each significant other had learned to live as his or her authentic self. I knew then that I had to launch the Self Vows program because it is not only needed by couples but is also essential for singles.

In addition, I have found that these programs also benefit married clients who haven't committed to self but whose attempt to commit to another first failed. So whether you're single or married, you can benefit from both programs. The Self Vows program will prepare you to take the vows to self first, and the Vows program will prepare you to take the vows to another and share all of you with the person you love.

From the response I received at the Self Vows Retreat, I knew I had uncovered and unleashed something very special. Once we launched the retreat (we don't have one for men yet, but we are working on it) and women were actively participating in the Self Vows program, along with pampering, sisterhood, deep reflection, and a life-changing ceremony, I knew I had to write this book. I needed to provide people with a blueprint for this new way of thinking about how we do our self-work.

My husband was supportive and instrumental as I wrote *The Vows* and *The Self Vows*. I didn't think I could write two books in the same year. Honestly, my confidence was a little low, and I was consumed with edits and content structure, so I wasn't my own biggest cheerleader. However, all it took was for my husband to say, "What about your self vows that you committed to? You have to share this with others." That was all I needed to hear to get into the writing. Through the whole process, between him, my spiritual brother Mike, and my support group, I was able to stay motivated.

Speaking of being committed to the vows, a woman who was thinking about getting married came into my office recently. She and her fiancé wanted to take the Vows program, but the meeting took a different turn. As I listened to her, I realized that she needed to take the self vows. Think about it. If you can't accept everything about yourself, meaning your flaws and the secrets that you hold dear to your heart, how can you do that for another person? To hold is to support, and support starts with you supporting yourself first, and then you are in position to support another. If you are stuck in past hurts and committed to holding onto the bondage of former situations, how will you be able to move forward with another? Again I ask, how can we take the vows to someone else when we haven't taken them for ourselves? My client took the vows to self and is continuing to do the work, and the more she evolved, the more she realized that marriage was not the right choice for her at that time. She wanted to spend some time dating, liking, forgiving, and loving herself.

It took years for me to get to the point where I had the courage to choose me and all that comes with that choice. Once I was becoming more confident in who I was, acceptance of the path that was unique to me was easier to take. After acting as a relationship broker for several corporate partnerships, I realized that the technique that was essential to my success was coaching and training. After completing my MBA and my master's degree in teaching and learning with technology, I made the decision to focus on relationship coaching. After a couple of years of gaining multiple certifications, I knew that my purpose was ready to be unleashed.

Who better could connect in a short period of time with the most closed-off individual? Who didn't mind introducing the tough conversations and guiding people through them in the most compassionate manner? Who could affect the world by decreasing the divorce rate and increasing the number of loving and healthy relationships? Who could create a program that would fit each and every unique individual? Who could provide people with a safe space to spiritually connect without any judgment regarding their religious choices? In the humblest energy, I realized that I was that person. I not only understood the complexities in relationships, but I was also willing to surrender to constant evolution, be transparent, and be vulnerable to going through each and every part of the process with my clients.

While my doctorate is in spiritual counseling and I identify with a Christian background, I respect all spiritual beliefs. Spiritual beliefs are very personal, and no one has the right to judge that special space in an individual's life.

After completing this book, I realized that it helped me stay motivated regarding my health challenges. It helped me recommit all over again to the "in sickness and in health" vow. It was not easy, but the more I wrote, the more deeply I opened up and fell in love with my depth of honesty.

ACKNOWLEDGMENTS

Father God, thank you for the gift of enlightenment on some of the most important vows. I love you!

Thanks to my parents for encouraging me to stay resilient no matter the obstacles.

Thank you to my mother for taking her self vows at seventy. It's the best gift you could have given me. It's the gift that keeps on giving the more you evolve.

Thank you to my husband for stepping out on faith and taking your self vows. You're blossoming, which means we're blossoming!

My daughter, I want nothing but happiness for you. Not for my dreams but for you to take the self vows and commit to the love of self first and foremost.

My grandma Nudie, who has birthed three generations of amazing, strong, and evolving women. My prayer is that before you leave this world, you take your self vows!

My best friends, Mike and Von, thank you for helping me on my journey to stand strong in taking the self vows. You are beyond a reason or season, but you all are my lifetimes. That's it. That's all.

Thank you to my best friend and sister friend Yolanda, who is one of the strongest women I know. A rare jewel comes close to describing you, but honestly, that still doesn't do you justice.

Thank you, Tommy, for loving and caring about someone that means the world to me. You have an amazing spirit!

Thank you to my sister circle—Michelle, Nekaya, and Tabz. Father God, you didn't forget about me; you gave me sisters.

A special thanks to Debbie and Michelle for ushering me into clarity!

To the women I have coached on how to take the vows and who, as a result, chose to live them daily, I am so proud of you.

To the ladies of the first Self Vows Retreat, thank you for being a part of the beginning!

Thank you to BBWR Network and Women Elevating Women for providing a platform for many women and businesses to shine, grow, and receive many resources that help women thrive and financially flourish.

Lastly, thank you to my production team: SnatchedbyP (makeup artist), Beauty by Kristen Payton (hair), Candice Arnold (CJA Virtual Assistant Services), and Beth Bruno (editor).

INTRODUCTION

This book is meant to be interactive. Knowing that many people are unable to travel for my one-on-one sessions, I want you to experience the feeling of being face-to-face with me as I take you through the program. In this spirit, the book contains tips and exercises that will guide you on your path of self-discovery.

The book walks you through each vow in a detailed way and pulls you into a state of mindfulness and reflection, chapter by chapter. *The Self Vows* is for anyone who has a desire to reflect more deeply, connect to the core of intimacy, and live authentically through a step-by-step process that uses the traditional wedding vows as a foundation to navigate through the process of ultimately committing to oneself. I chose the traditional wedding vows because I feel they unearth the truth of who we are, who we strive to be, and who we can become in the closest relationship two people can share. They act as a mirror of what our lives should reflect daily. *The Self Vows: Seven Vows That Will Change Your Life* includes stories to illustrate key concepts as well as exercises to follow. I have faith in you that, after reading this book, you will commit to the self vows as a daily inner compass as it relates to you being healthy, happy, healed, and consistently authentic. Don't you think it's time to change your life and reset all that doesn't serve you? You can do it. Well, you're already doing it because you took the first step: you bought this book.

If you need to learn how to have and support everything about yourself or others, if you need to learn how to stop looking in the rearview mirror and move forward, if you want to learn how to commit to yourself and others or how to have a healthy relationship with finances while working through and forgiving unhealthy financial choices, you must continue reading. If you have a desire for a love that connects to daily evolution, happiness, and freedom, commit to this book of love. Finally, first and foremost, you will learn and accept that you will never leave you. When you commit to self in that way, you will find it much easier to commit to another.

I give you ultimate transparency in this book. My desire is to connect to you through my journey, the journeys of others, and well-thought-out questions that will penetrate deep within if you allow them to. I commit to taking this journey with you. Every time you open this book, it symbolizes me showing up to guide you through a path that can be a most difficult one. On the other hand, it will be the most amazing journey you will ever experience. You are the most important priority because without your peace of mind, everything else is meaningless. There's no rush. Be patient and allow yourself to feel all feelings. Surrender to healing, and I promise when you get to the end, you will not be the same person. I can't wait for you to meet your authentic self. Be well and loved, my friend.

Here are a few rules for answering the questions in this book:

- Read the questions, breathe, and answer truthfully. If you don't know the answer, circle back at a later time.
- Instead of taking the easy way out and answering with a yes or no, delve deeper and elaborate on why you feel the way you do and where the feelings come from. Provide evidence for your answers. Challenge yourself.
- At the end of each chapter, there will be tips and exercises that will help you dig a little deeper and provide an opportunity to put what you have learned into action.

These tough questions are meant to open up a dialogue, change the trajectory of your path, help you make sound and healthy decisions, and provide a deeper understanding of the relationship with self and how the self vows apply to your daily life. These questions are meant to provide clarity, peace, happiness, balance, and love that you deserve.

The love notes throughout the book provide different perspectives for you to consider before and after answering the questions. They also trigger a deeper reflection and provide you with a virtual coach: *me*.

And finally, the personal stories at the end of the book are a bonus from some very important people (clients and family) who have trusted me with their amazing self vows journeys.

CHAPTER 1

To Have and to Hold from This Day Forward

What does it mean to take the self vows? Imagine giving yourself the greatest gift a person can give him- or herself outside the spiritual connection we have to God, which is the foundation of who we are. We spend half our lives wanting and waiting to take the traditional wedding vows with someone else, but we are unaware that we need to take the vows to self first. So many people stand before God, the minister, and congregation and commit to some of the most important vows one can take, without truly knowing the magnitude of power, honor, respect, vulnerability, and choice to love and give of ourselves to another that comes with them.

In order to truly give of ourselves to another, we have to understand and give everything about us to ourselves first. God gives us the gift of life, and it is only right that, in gratitude, we take that life and honor it, have compassion for it, and use it for its divine purpose. It's a process to get to a place to like, fall in love with, and love *yourself* through pain, fear, joy, and triumphs.

But first, there are some steps we have to take before taking the self vows. My four B principles will help you lay the groundwork so that you are well-equipped to answer and reflect on the questions in the following chapters.

The Four Bs

The four Bs are breakup, breakdown, breakthrough and breakout. My first book, *The Breaking Point: A Full Circle Journey*, addresses the phases of the four Bs. The four

Bs will help you make conscious choices and help you live a deliberate life. They will facilitate your understanding of how to live every day beyond fear, pain, brokenness, and disappointment. The four Bs can help anyone in his or her personal or business relationships. For the purposes of this book, we will focus on the personal relationships, but the four Bs have helped both individuals and businesses to transform and live authentically. The four Bs have changed people's lives by meeting them in crisis and ushering them into peace and living their best lives.

Being intentional about the results you want to achieve while moving through this process is essential to your success. Be intentional about breaking up from toxicity, breaking down the barriers, breaking through fear and pain, and breaking out into your purpose. If you keep your intentions in alignment with the four Bs, you will begin to answer the important questions not only from a deeper perspective but also from a place of evolution.

Breakup

When we think about the word *breakup*, we usually associate it with the end of a relationship with a boyfriend or girlfriend. But sometimes it's necessary to break up with self in order to unleash our authentic selves. As I stated previously, it is absolutely necessary to divorce the false self if we are to marry the self that we are destined to be—the authentic self. Breaking up from toxicity can be challenging when we are used to being in relationships full of it. Haven't you ever wondered why certain people stay in abusive relationships? Well, we can also be in a toxic relationship with self and be stuck in the pain of it. We know that we need to make a change, but we just can't seem to figure out the first step to take. By the way, *breakup* contains the word *up*, so why not take a different perspective and focus on the *up*? Sometimes we know the steps but still can't move to action. Here are some steps to help you get started:

1. Delete. Get rid of the things about you that don't serve you anymore. Delete the lies that people have told you or that you told yourself. In order to start the process of detoxifying relationships with others, we have to start with ourselves. Make a list of all the things you know that make you feel the opposite of good. Repeat this step until you feel that you have truly evaluated every relationship in your life. Doing that gives you a chance to reflect after each time. You will know when it feels right to finalize the list. Make the choice to start deleting the items one by one. Keep in mind that relationships of the past may still carry painful feelings. I believe that you can't delete feelings, but you can let go of the pain and make

the choice to heal. Some relationships might need to be deleted for a season and not a lifetime. Nevertheless, you must do it, especially if it will bring you peace.

2. Reset. The word *reset* is defined as setting something again or putting something back to zero. We don't want to go back to zero because our past and present serve as life lessons and give us the opportunity to evolve. We want to concentrate on setting something again. I believe a reset is a do-over. A do-over is an opportunity to do something differently than you did the first time around. The do-over is the lesson you've learned and the different perspective you've gained since the first time. Once you delete and reset you are ready for a restructure. The beautiful thing is you can reset as many times as you need to. Remember it's your life.

3. Restructure. Restructuring is defined as a reorganization or a shake-up, and that is exactly what you have to commit to doing next. So let the shaking begin. Shake off the things that cause you consistent pain: disappointments, defeats, self-sabotage, negative self-talk, and low self-esteem. Once you start to shake these things off, start reorganizing your life one step at a time. The key word is *change*. Take everything you have chosen to shake off and replace it with things that serve you and bring you a balanced and healthy life.

Breakdown

It is time to surrender to authenticity and break down barriers. At this point, you are tired of feeling like you are in pieces and are now ready to humble yourself, open your heart, and surrender to your truth. We resist most what we need to surrender to. Barriers are difficult to break down when we are unaware of what they are. Identifying what prevents you from getting unstuck is key.

Think about what you would be doing if you were not scared of failing or rejection. I'm sure it would feel freeing if the barrier of fear was deleted, so start reflecting on your barriers. As you go through this book chapter by chapter, ask yourself what or who is preventing you from committing to this vow? Identify what is preventing you from surrendering to your purpose and authenticity. Whatever the answer and no matter what the vow, I guarantee it will show itself. You can't run from fear, but you can make the choice to face it. Open your heart and just let the process happen organically.

Breakthrough

A breakthrough is defined as an important discovery or a removal of barriers in order to progress. Once you begin to live authentically, you will begin to experience many self-discoveries. Living authentically means coming from a genuine place and being disconnected from being anything other than who you are. You are committed to living in your truth no matter what that truth makes others feel. You are determined not to connect to a lie even if that lie was told to you by people you respect.

I have been told many things that I accepted as gospel without my own research or process of self-discovery. I just believed it because I felt the person who told me knew best, and I dared not question it. I realized that I was just scared to trust my own thoughts. Well, truthfully, I didn't even know what most of my thoughts were. I never got to know myself; I was too busy getting to know everyone else. I honestly was just begging for people to see me and validate my worthiness. Does this sound like you at all? If so, it's time to start living authentically, and to do that you must break down the barriers and break through the fear that prevents you from taking that journey.

You can't break through without deleting the toxic relationships, surrendering, and doing your own self-work. Remember you can't spell breakthrough without spelling *break* and *rough*. It is necessary for you to experience a break, to feel that your life is breaking into pieces. If your life never fell apart, there would be no need to go through the lessons that lead to the choice of putting it back together. Putting it back together results in a breakthrough.

For some people who are feeling broken into pieces and damaged, the result is being stuck. However, if you acknowledge that you are broken and that you have allowed trials to damage you but you are willing to do something different, you have realized that restructuring your self-worth and identifying your value are key to confirming that you are ready for a breakthrough.

Breakout

You are no longer stuck or in pain. You are now free to be you and can explore and unleash your purpose. However, you cannot fully identify your purpose if you are trying to define it from a lie. If you are not living within your truth, it's impossible to truly break out and unleash your purpose. Your purpose is why you exist. It's what brings joy to you and others. Some have the pleasure of their livelihoods being their purpose, and to me, that's one of the greatest blessings. It doesn't feel like work when you love what you do.

Don't put pressure on yourself to know your purpose. When you organically begin to live authentically, I promise purpose will follow right behind. It actually will become obvious and will confirm itself over and over again.

Now that you have set the stage with the four Bs as the foundation of self-reflection and an inner compass to help you work through each chapter, you are prepared and ready to start the process of taking the self vows. Remember to be patient; this is a process, and everyone's process is different. The quicker you make the choice to begin, the closer you are to living as your authentic self.

Your self vows under God the Father are the most important vows you will ever make. Taking these vows to yourself first will make it easier to commit to another person. So take the vows and wait for the extension of love—the one—to show up. I promise he or she will. I am a living witness.

To Have and to Hold from This Day Forward

Have everything about yourself. What I mean by this is own your genius; your flaws; your cellulite; your past, present, and future; and your inner and outer beauty. Hold your mind, body, and soul in the highest regard. For example, you might consider taking pride in your body and choosing to be celibate or at least not to sleep with someone who doesn't share your convictions about the sacredness of physical intimacy. Celibacy is a pretty good choice, considering it means zero chance of contracting sexually transmitted diseases and avoids the confusion that sometimes comes when we introduce sex into a new relationship.

To hold means to support you even if sometimes you don't understand you. You see, when you make each of the self vows, you commit to the vow no matter what. Supporting your dreams, visions, and goals is essential to reach your full potential. When things seem the worst and no one is around to be your cheerleader, tell you it will be okay, or give you the biggest hug ever, the support you need has always been there. It's within you. Show up for you! Hold up your beliefs. Not anyone else's—just yours.

The Author's Story

Having everything about myself was the hardest thing I have ever had to do. I had to strip down and tell the truth. The truth is that I didn't want anyone to know. I was terrified to speak it. The truth was many things, but at the core of it all was the fact that I didn't know me and I definitely didn't like the imposter who had settled in for years. The imposter was what other people wanted or expected me to be. I started to realize that as I began to sit and write the things I liked to do and how I liked to feel. I was challenged by one question: Is this what I truly like, or is it what my family, friends, society, and social media like or want me to like? I was at a crossroads, and I wanted to meet every bit of me. I was ready to face the challenging parts and discover the beauty in me.

The first step was going through the process of the four Bs. Once I conquered implementing them daily in my personal and business life, I was prepared for the work needed to embrace authenticity. I was ready to dive deep into exploring who I was. I realized that, at that time, I was fear. Most things about me were fearful. I thought to myself, *How could I have had so much courage yet experience so much fear daily?* The what-ifs were horrible … What if people don't like me? What if they don't accept me? What if I'm not enough? What if I never reach major success? What if I never make my mother happy? What if I never get mother of the year? What if I never have a successful relationship? What if I never know the real me? The last question was the one that actually pushed me to continue even more deeply in my self-work after writing my first book. I realized that the first book was about me facing my pain and accepting accountability for my actions and feelings. It was disconnecting from the blame game. Quite frankly, I'd thought I was done. I had never done self-work like that before, but that was only the beginning.

The second step was looking in the mirror every day and asking myself to have the thing about myself that I tried to cover up or replace with a lie. For example, a lie: "Your writing is in vain, no one cares, and not enough people are embracing your books." My answer of courage: "I am patient, I will have every fear and impatient feeling that comes from within me, and I embrace my books and everything that goes into them."

On the other hand, just because I have even the negative things about myself doesn't mean that I won't embrace the shift that is needed to change to positive thoughts. Many leaders have reported that it takes five seconds to change a thought, maybe less. If you begin to let thoughts linger past five seconds, more negative thoughts will come. This started to change my entire outlook on how I see myself.

Another thing that was hard for me to have about myself was my sensitivity. Instead of accepting it, I tried to be the opposite, which came off as cold at times. I had to realize the truth: I am sensitive and that's what connects to people who are hurting and need compassion. Eventually, I began to have more and more about who I was at that time.

The third step was standing in my truth and having pride about who I am and that I am happy to have me. Know that when you stand in your truth, people will try to convince you that you are someone else or provide so many reasons you shouldn't have everything about yourself. I find that when you walk in your truth, it challenges others to confront their own truths. Either they embrace it and want to embrace that same light, or they run from it because they are more comfortable with living in their lies.

I made a choice to be vulnerable to you and share my journey. Will you be vulnerable with yourself and implement the four Bs process and embrace the steps to having everything about yourself? The questions below will help you peel back the layers and gain a new perspective of self.

Self Vows Questions

Identity

1. Who are you?

   Love note: Use nouns, not adjectives, to answer this question. For example: I am peace, I am happiness, I am anger. Please reflect deeply on who you are in this moment, not who you want to be. Who we are manifests in our relationships through decisions and actions. If you are fear, then your choices and decisions will be made from a place of fear. Explain your answer.

2. Am I content with who I am? If not, what needs to be changed?

   Love note: If you are content but know that change is needed, you are accepting something about yourself or someone that doesn't serve you.

3. Am I committed to evolving?

   Love note: Evolution is a gradual process. Patience is essential while going through the process to achieve a healthy lifestyle, both mentally and physically.

4. Am I an honest or a deceitful person?

   Love note: If you are dishonest with yourself, everything you do will have traces of a lie.

5. Am I motivated in the areas that are important to me? I motivate myself by … (fill in the blank).

   Love note: If you don't do things you like and enjoy doing, you won't stay motivated.

6. Am I a coward or a person with courage?

   Love note: Both fear and courage are contagious. The choice is yours. If you choose courage, you will attract just that.

7. Do I abuse myself or others?
   Love note: Physical abuse, emotional abuse, and drug abuse are common forms of abuse. But you should also consider other types of abuse such as self-sabotage, negative self-talk, and self-inflicted physical abuse.

8. Do I have integrity?
   Love note: A person with integrity says, "I will do what's right even when no one is looking." Integrity and sneakiness cannot go hand in hand. Even if no one saw something you did with wrong intentions, you know. The worst kind of betrayal is the one of self.

9. Do I always have to be right, or am I more concerned with getting right?
   Love note: Many times we just want to win an argument instead of resolving the issue (getting it right). Knowledge speaks, but wisdom listens. Both are needed.

10. Do I have determination, or am I easily defeated? How is my life affected by this?
    Love note: There is no defeat unless we give up on God. Remember the mind is powerful, and even if you don't feel it in this moment, your mind is strong.

11. Am I broken or whole? Broken is the person who holds you responsible for defining the greatness in him or her. Whole is when you have already defined the greatness in you, and only then can you share it with another.
    Love note: Being broken can sometimes be the best gift and teacher. If we are open, we will learn the greatest lesson while we are in the *break* of it all.

Support

1. Do I lift myself up, or do I tear myself down?
   Love note: Focus on your intentions for saying or doing certain things. Intentions affect our actions and the results.

2. What does it mean for me to move forward? Who and what do you need to leave in the past?
   Love note: When you keep looking in the rearview mirror instead of forward through the windshield—the biggest window in the car—you increase your chance of crashing, and some crashes can be deadly!

3. How do I protect myself?

   Love note: Protecting self means keeping self away from any emotional or physical harm. Protecting ourselves also requires us to identify negative people in our lives. If we identify negative people, we can then make a conscious decision to distance ourselves from the negativity. Where does that negativity come from? Insecurity? Envy? A distinct dissatisfaction with life? We can also protect ourselves by guarding against negative self-talk.

4. What do I do to pick myself up when I fall? Is it effective?

   Love note: Falling is such a motivation to get back up again. Failure scares people, so they often fail to act on their dreams and ambitions. Failure will humble you. Failure is often the result of fear of change. Change brings the unknown, which in turn forces us out of our comfort zones.

5. How do I support myself?

   Love note: We have to support ourselves first before we can support others.

6. Am I constantly distracted, or am I fully present?

   Love note: Distractions could be work, multi-tasking, TV, or being consumed with social media. When we are distracted, we miss the lessons or the gifts that surround us.

7. Am I a support or a toxic vampire?

   Love note: A toxic vampire is someone who sucks the energy from you consistently. If you feel this way, it might be safe to say that you or the person with whom you are in a relationship is a toxic vampire. Taking a hard look at ourselves is essential if we are to improve our positive outlook on life, work, and our relationships. If you identify yourself as a toxic vampire, just know that you can delete those behaviors and reset new ones.

Active Listening

While self-talk is very important, listening is even the more so. Before a thought even forms, we hear that inner voice first, and then we speak what we have heard.

Active listening involves listening with all your senses. "As well as giving one's full attention to the speaker, it is important that the active listener is also seen to be listening; otherwise, the speaker could conclude that what he or she is talking about is uninteresting to the listener" ("Active Listening," *Skills You Need,* https://www.skillsyouneed.com/ips/active-listening.html).

When I think of communication, listening is the foundation of communicating effectively. Listening doesn't just innately happen; that is hearing. Listening, on the other hand, is an active process that is a choice we make. We choose to want to understand the message of the speaker.

To be an effective and good listener, one has to remain nonjudgmental and neutral, and disconnect from being close-minded. It's difficult to not form opinions, take sides, or interject our own perspective, whether nonverbally or verbally, before an individual finishes his or her statement. Active listening is also about patience; pauses and short periods of silence should be accepted. Impatient listeners interrupt consistently. How irritating and frustrating is that for the individual attempting to convey his or her thoughts? Listeners should not be tempted to jump in with questions or comments every time there are a few seconds of silence. Active listening involves giving the other person adequate time to explore his or her thoughts and feelings. People who are in the habit of jumping in tend to be selfish listeners and truly have one agenda, which is for them to be heard and not to truly listen with compassion.

I have received so many messages just by listening. Remember knowledge speaks, but wisdom listens. When you are distracted, you don't fully get the message and therefore don't learn the lesson. Be fully present and you will always get a gift or, most importantly, give a gift.

Tips for Better Active Listening

- Recap. Repeating what you believe you have heard back to the person you're listening to will ensure that both of you are clear.
- Summarize. Summarizing the entire conversation at the end will guarantee that the other party knows you have acknowledged what they said, validated it, and shown compassion for what they just shared. Summarizing is different than recapping in the sense that it encompasses the entire conversation, including any clarifications from the recap.
- Use encouraging words. Using positive prompts encourages the other party to feel that he or she is in a safe environment. For example, you might say, "Uh-huh" or "Oh?" or "I understand." "Then?" and "And?" are also effective.
- Reflect. Make sure that in addition to recapping you reflect on the speaker's words as it relates to his or her feelings. For example, you could say, "This seems really crucial to you …"

- Give feedback. Once you have your initial thoughts regarding the situation, share pertinent information and your own observations, insights, and experiences. Make sure that your initial thoughts consist of healthy reflection and openness.
- Ask probing questions. Ask the right questions to motivate the individual to go deeper and have a more meaningful conversation. Try not to start questions with why or ask leading questions.
- Use pauses effectively. Deliberately pause at key points for emphasis. This will tell the person that you are saying something very important.
- Be silent. Silence is sometimes the most beautiful gift you can give someone when it comes to listening. It slows down the exchange and gives you both a time to think instead of talk.
- Use "I" messages. By using "I" in your statements, you focus on the problem, not the person. An "I" message lets the person know what you feel and why. For example, "I know you have a lot to say, but I need to …"

Self-Talk—The Negative and Positive

The inner voice that you have within is defined as self-talk. It's an inner monologue that runs throughout the day and sometimes keeps you up at night. What is your inner voice speaking to you daily? Do you know? This inner voice consists of conscious and unconscious thoughts. It's an effective way for the brain to interpret and process daily experiences.

This voice is useful when it is positive, talking down fears and enhancing confidence. However, when it's negative, it can change the entire trajectory of our lives. Human nature is prone to negative self-talk. However, statements like "I'm always messing up" or "I will never be successful" tend to keep us stuck and on the opposite path of reaching our full potential. On the other hand, if you become aware of the negative self-talk, you can choose to turn your way of thinking around and infuse it with positive thoughts.

Positive self-talk can enhance your performance and general well-being. For example, I lost all my edits and the wind was knocked out of me. I had added more than ten thousand words of new sections during the editing phase. My computer crashed, and it was gone. I cried, I grieved, and I honored what had been lost. Finally, I moved from feeling lost into positive self-talk for the next eight hours. I am a witness that it does wonders for your outcome. Obviously it works, because you are reading this.

Positive self-talk has several benefits:

- increased energy
- greater life satisfaction
- reduced pain
- better cardiovascular health
- more days of happiness and health
- better physical well-being
- healthy decisions
- reduced risk for death
- less stress

Meanwhile, negative self-talk can affect us in some pretty destructive ways. Just look around at the state of the world, whether it's your family, strangers, or just globally. We need to commit to positive self-talk daily.

Studies have linked negative self-talk with higher levels of stress and lower levels of self-esteem. This can lead to unhealthy relationships, decreased motivation, and greater feelings of hopelessness. This type of critical inner dialogue in many correlates to mental disorders, specifically depression. Think about it: if we fix the negative self-talk, we could be having a healthy self-concept, which would result in increased transparency and enhanced intimacy in our relationships with self and others.

People who find themselves frequently engaging in negative self-talk tend to be convinced that this is their reality. They don't understand that all it takes is a few steps in changing the limited thinking, disconnecting from perfectionism, and being open to different perspectives as it relates to life's challenges. Being stuck blinds you to opportunities around you and decreases the ability to capitalize on those opportunities. If you are stuck in negative self-talk, your goals are often at risk of not being completed.

There are numerous consequences of negative self-talk:

- limited beliefs
- lack of productivity
- problematic communication
- lack of clarity
- relationship challenges
- not reaching your full potential

You may be asking yourself, "How do I change my way of thinking?" Of course I have some tips and steps to get you started. Being aware of the items listed in the following pages, reflecting on them, and having a compassionate, factual self-talk conversation will get you started toward debunking the negative feelings that are outright lies and seeing things you deem negative in a different perspective. Remember nothing happens overnight. Just as you practice negative self-talk, choose to practice awareness by executing these tips and reflective questioning daily.

Here are some actions that lead to consistent negative self-talk:

- self-blame
  Reflective question: Where might your perception of yourself be wrong?
  Tip: Identify negative self-talk traps.

- catastrophizing most situations
  Reflective question: Do your thoughts define you? Is your perception of the situation fact or feeling?
  Tip: Check in with your feelings.

- polarizing perspective of the world
  Reflective question: Do you find yourself always saying never or always? Nothing is ever always or never … Remember being reflective and open means having different perspectives.
  Tip: Find the humor.

- magnifying the negative instead of the positive
  Reflective question: Are you scared of what the positive could change in your life? Do you find comfort in the negative thinking?
  Tip: Surround yourself with positive people. Give yourself positive affirmations.

If you are confused about the difference between negative and positive self-talk, here are a few examples:

Negative: I'm fat and I'm never going to lose weight. I might as well give up.
Positive: I am capable and strong, and I am committed to being healthier for me.

Negative: I let everyone on my team down when I didn't close the deal.
Positive: Collaboration or partnerships work as a team, which is not *I* but *we*. We win and lose together.

Negative: I can't change my mind. People will be disappointed.
Positive: I have the right to change my mind, and I give myself permission. Whomever will understand.

Negative: I'm a failure and embarrassed myself.
Positive: I celebrate my life and I honor my efforts. That took courage.

Negative: I've never done this before and I'll fail at it.
Positive: I welcome this opportunity for me to learn from others and grow.

Negative: There's no way this will work. I'm not smart enough.
Positive: I can and will give it my all to make it work.

Positive self-talk takes practice if it's not your natural instinct. If you're generally more pessimistic, you can learn to shift your inner dialogue to be more encouraging and uplifting. If you find that the tips or being consistently aware and self-reflecting aren't enough for you to start feeling healthy, perhaps you need one-on-one coaching in addition to seeing a therapist. It's okay to reach out to a professional. Remember you are so needed in this world, but you need you first.

Self Vows Questions

Communication

1. Is my self-talk positive and gentle?
    Love note: Screaming suggests people are emotionally far apart. If you scream at yourself, what does that say about your *self* relationship? When the tone is gentle, people are less defensive.

2. Do I listen to myself? What listening techniques do I use (e.g., active listening, restatement, mirroring, staying in the present, acknowledgement of the thoughts of others, etc.)?
    Love note: Listening is the skill that allows you to master personal and professional greatness.

3. Do I listen with compassion or with lack of concern?

Love note: Our facial expressions—positive and negative—communicate a lot to others. In addition, multitasking when someone is communicating something important suggests you are not fully engaged therefore, it is not a healthy attribute in a relationship.

4. Do I communicate by shutting down? If so, what's the outcome? Does it resolve anything?
   Love note: Avoidance, rejection, or judgments are all reasons for shutting down, but love of self is the one reason you shouldn't.

5. Do I journal? Does it work for me?
   Love note: There are many ways to journal, but make sure you tell your truth. Read for clarity, change the things that need changed, make a self-care plan, and execute it.

6. Am I a poor communicator or someone who is open and in touch with my feelings? How does this make me feel?
   Love note: A poor communicator often has no interest in learning how to engage with a different communication style or determining if they can. A poor communicator often walks away when he or she gets frustrated because he or she is having challenges with articulating feelings or factual information. Someone who always answers yes, no, or I don't know with no explanation is a poor communicator. If this sounds like you, it's time for a change!

Commitment

1. Am I available, body and soul?
   Love note: Available in body means monogamous, while available in soul means spiritually connected.

2. Am I committed to self-care? Am I devoted to the responsibility that comes along with achieving a healthy self-care regimen?
   Love note: Self-care can include good nutrition, an effective exercise plan, and a deep connection with your spiritual self.

3. Do I attempt to hide secrets from myself?
   Love note: Isn't it funny how we try to hide secrets from ourselves? Once you are open and vulnerable with yourself, hiding from self is not an option.

Spirituality

1. Explain your spiritual connection. What are your spiritual views?
    Love note: It's okay to explore and welcome your own spiritual journey. Remember this is very intimate and personal; no one can tell you how to be intimate with your God.

From this Day Forward

This part of the vow is associated with moving ahead and progressing. It indicates improvement. Once you make up your mind to have everything and support yourself, this is the next step. It's taking everything that you learned about self, showing up in the world, and presenting who you are. It's not looking back but pushing forward. Moving forward is welcoming the daily uncovering of self and the natural progression of growth.

Moving forward can sometimes feel like grieving the old self. It's tough to bury the past and wake up every morning ready to conquer the day with hope, love, and enthusiasm. However, once you have made up your mind to truly be present, it's not difficult at all to be committed to moving forward.

Self Vows Questions

Moving Forward

1. Am I constantly bringing up the past?
    Love note: Bringing up the past constantly is a sign that you have not forgiven yourself, and that is unhealthy. You can't begin something new when you are determined to hold on to the old!

2. What does it mean for me if I choose to stay in the past?
    Love note: Staying in the past will determine the pace for how you move forward. People cling to the past because it's familiar, even if it's painfully familiar. People cling to the past because it feels safe. If we cling to the past, we cannot possibly move forward. Instead, we'll remain lost in the negativity. If you think about it, most people don't wallow in the past with wonderful memories. They are almost always negative.

3. Do I unfairly blame my ex-partner for the present status of my life?
    Love note: Baggage from a past relationship should be acknowledged, dealt with, and healed before you enter a new relationship.

4. Do I move toward my goals and vision, or do I push them away by moving backward?

   Love note: Imagine you've been walking on a long road and you are a step away from true freedom, but then you look back and allow part of your past to paralyze you. What seemed so close is now far away because you are stuck. This is what happens when you continue to look back: the past holds your freedom hostage.

5. How have I learned from past relationships, and how do these lessons help me succeed in future relationships?

   Love note: Past relationships can be challenging to reflect on, but it's a welcoming thought when you have learned a lesson. Lessons are our greatest teachers. The ones that have hurt us the most have taught us something great about ourselves.

6. What is my relationship with forgiveness? Is it healthy (I find it easy to forgive) or unhealthy (I hold grudges for days, months, or years)?

   Love note: Remember you have the choice to unhook yourself from the anchor of unforgiveness. Freedom is not a hook in your back.

Communication

1. How do I deal with disagreements?

   Love note: The way you approach conflict determines whether your disagreements are toxic or healthy.

2. How do I define my communication style? Am I indirect or direct? Am I a yeller or soft-spoken? Am I the abandoner (walks away from conversation) or the one who gets abandoned (left standing in the middle of a conversation)? Am I the insider (holds everything inside) or the outsider (wears feelings on my sleeve)?

   Love note: Defining your style will help you communicate more effectively and be aware of what you need to improve.

3. Do I promote myself in a positive way? Is the image I present truthful, or am I upholding the image of what I would *like* to be the truth?

   Love note: Often we are scared to be truthful that we might be in trouble or pain. We are hesitant to be totally transparent to our friends and family because we fear that we may disappoint them. With that said, we hide behind a lie (the image) and project that everything is wonderful. I'm not suggesting you should tell just anyone your personal business, but you should be mindful of your intentions.

Vulnerability

1. Am I ready for my relationship with self to evolve, or am I set in my ways?
   Love note: I like to think of love as a pair of glasses that magnify the areas in which we need to evolve.

Kyler's Story

Throughout my life, I have always sought out validation. Most people like to be reassured and validated, but there is a healthy and unhealthy way to receive either. Looking back, I went about seeking both in the wrong way and looked for it in the wrong places. It wasn't until last year that I finally just said, "If you can't love every part of me, then you aren't worth my time." I finally stopped being a "yes girl" and found the true power of *no*. I realized that if you can't have and accept every part of me, you're not worth my time. I was aware that I had to have everything about me and start doing things for Kyler.

My mom has frequently expressed that you teach people how to treat you, and that's exactly what I'm doing—teaching people how to treat me. It feels freeing to know and unapologetically confess that I come first. I had to have everything about me in order to create a positive and peaceful mind-set for self. I had to work on myself by myself. I couldn't bring anyone into that space because it was a self-learning process.

One thing that stands out about my journey, to have and accept, was my hair. It may sound silly to some, but to most women of color, it is a very real concern. Being African American, you realize early on that hair is very important. I heard the terms *good hair* and *bad hair and* felt I fell between the two. Why did I have to choose? Why couldn't it be my hair, good or bad? My hair wasn't long, and culturally that was considered unattractive (at least that was my experience). I wore weaves and braids, but there was a part of me that just wanted to be free and rock my natural hair. I wanted that to be okay.

I began to ask myself questions daily: What did being okay mean? Who did I want to be in my space? What qualities did I need to work on? What did happy feel like and look like? I reflected on those questions day in and day out. Some questions were answered, but as I evolved, my answers did too.

In 2016, I "went natural" for the first time since early childhood. I never really wore my natural hair; it was constantly being straightened into various styles. When I decided to try it, I guess I couldn't fully commit to the process of taking care of my hair. In addition, products needed for natural styles were expensive, and a college kid had to eat. I found it was easier to just get a protective style because my hair would be a big poof within a couple of days. It was a cycle. I would get so fed up with trying to style my natural hair that many times I gave up.

Since then, I have had an epiphany: anything worth having is worth the process, whether long or short. I guess I have to commit to the process to get a different result. Just as I reflected on questions about self, I can ask questions about my hair. Doesn't my hair deserve to know me and me it? What does my hair need? What type of hair do I have? What foods could help me to have healthier hair? I decided to have a relationship with self, and my hair is a part of me. I'm now looking forward to getting to know my hair.

Being your own cheerleader is not always easy, but I have developed a certain love for myself that no one can take away from me. When I am feeling down, I have learned to find the things that get me out of that rut. For example, taking hot showers, taking a drive around the neighborhood, or even watching a funny show are some of the things that make me relax, calm down, and smile. If I went through my life wanting or waiting for people to congratulate or be there for me, I would probably be very sad. Even my very best friends can be unreliable sometimes, and I have to be okay with that because I realize they have their own lives as well. I have to know myself and learn how to be the best version of me.

I have learned "to have" everything about myself emotionally, physically, and spiritually. I value my body, and I know my self worth is priceless. I hold (support) myself in the challenging times and the triumphs because I realize that when you are your first supporter no matter what, you are exercising "to hold." I constantly move on without letting the past control me. I do that by never regretting anything and instead making everything a learning experience. Whether a moment was good or challenging, it happened. There is no use letting something control my life that already happened. I accept it, figure out what I learned, and use it for next time. I commit to moving forward!

Let's Get Ready to Do Your Work

Exercise 1: Let's Air This Dirty Laundry

Some of us wait for weeks before we do our laundry. Others do laundry weekly. Then there's the folding and putting the clothes away, and that may be extended to a week or two. Similarly, many of us wait to do our self-relationship laundry for weeks, months, or years. We all know that when laundry piles up for weeks, it starts to stink, and the longer we wait, the more challenging it is to get out stains. In fact, the stains can become permanent. It's the same process with you. When you ignore issues such as irritations and unspoken resentments, toxic behaviors start to "stain" you. The longer we wait to address the stains, the more likely it is that the relationship will suffer permanent damage. If you take the steps in this exercise, you and your partner will have a much healthier connection.

- Step 1: Wash clothes weekly (address issues).
- Step 2: Separate colors from whites (colors are more complex issues; whites are lighter issues).
- Step 3: Dry clothes (generate options for resolution).
- Step 4: Fold clothes immediately after they're dry (strategize a plan and reflect on possible resolutions).
- Step 5: Put clothes away (resolve challenges and renew your self-commitment daily).

Exercise 2: I Feel …

Expressing our feelings can be difficult at times, especially when we are angry. Often the communication is full of "you" statements that tend to put you in a space (e.g., "You are not good enough!" or "You never will achieve success!"). Using "I" statements instead can prevent an unhealthy breakdown in communication. Instead of "You are not good enough," try, "I feel not valued when I feel judged, which makes me feel not good enough." Instead of saying, "I never will achieve success," try "I feel defeated when I continue to fail, which makes me feel like I will not achieve success."

Blaming yourself for variables outside of your control is unfair and unkind to self, and it could result in depression, feeling stuck, or low self-esteem. You can express your feelings about yourself without tearing down your self-esteem. Expressing yourself clearly prevents the assumptions and negative self-talk.

Practice using this "I" statement frame:

I feel_____ because _____ when _____.

Reflective Notes

Reflective Notes

Reflective Notes

CHAPTER 2

Authenticity: The Freedom I Never Had!

Authenticity is not a race. It's a journey to know who *you* are. According to Stephen Joseph, PhD, authenticity is defined as the attempt to live one's life according to the needs of one's inner being, rather than the demands of society or one's early conditioning.[1] Authenticity is ultimately about the qualities that show healthy, nondefensive functioning and psychological maturity.

Here are some characteristics of authenticity:

- ✓ Being realistic.
- ✓ Accepting yourself and others in your and their present state.
- ✓ Being thoughtful of your needs instead of putting yourself last.
- ✓ Having a sense of humor that is not intentionally meant to hurt.
- ✓ Being open, clear, and transparent about your feelings.
- ✓ Being open to learning from your mistakes and restructuring your life.

On the other hand, here is what not being authentic looks like:

- ✓ Being self-deceptive and unrealistic in your perceptions of reality.

---

[1] Stephen Joseph, "7 Qualities of Truly Authentic People," *What Doesn't Kill Us* (blog), *Psychology Today*, August 29, 2016, https://www.psychologytoday.com/us/blog/what-doesnt-kill-us/201608/7-qualities-truly-authentic-people.

✓ Looking to public opinion to validate your actions and feelings.
✓ Being judgmental of self.
✓ Not thinking clearly through your thoughts.
✓ Having a hostile sense of humor toward self.
✓ Inability to express your emotions freely and clearly because of fear.
✓ Not being open to learning from your mistakes.

Joseph goes on to say, "If behind what a person says and does is a defensive and self-deceptive approach to life, then no matter how passionate and committed he or she is to a cause, ultimately that person is not being true to him or herself."

When your heart is open and you are vulnerable without apology, you will be able to

- define who you are through exercising self-love;
- exhibit self-concept, self-belief, and self-acceptance;
- love who you are;
- determine your life purpose; and
- live authentically.

Define Who You Are

It may be a hard pill to swallow, but it's entirely possible that some of the things you believe about yourself aren't true at all! It's necessary to visit the past and reflect on how it has affected your self-concept while on your quest toward your authentic self.

Everyone carries around negative experiences of the past. Some of these experiences were our own fault, while others were not. What's most relevant is how these experiences are interpreted. Feelings are relevant to our experiences, specifically how we interpret them. It's challenging not to assign meaning to those experiences, but the question we need to ask ourselves is if those feelings accurate or useful.

If you are not using your past constructively, you will find yourself lying, making the same mistakes, and adopting many negative aspects of your parents and beliefs you didn't choose for yourself. From the past, we learn what serves us and what doesn't, provided the experience is interpreted correctly. If you ignore the past, healing will not occur. If there is something in your past that you choose to fight hard to forget, then something about that situation is hurting you in the present. When you are healed of something, it doesn't hurt anymore.

If you have adopted negative aspects from your parents, then you know that it has affected the trajectory of your life. For example, do you lie like your father did? Do you self-medicate like your mother did? Do you tear your partner down like one of your parents did? Do you get yourself in debt time after time like your father? Do you choose abusive relationships like one of your parents did? Do you judge other races based on what you heard your parents say and do? Perhaps none of these examples reflect your parents. Perhaps it was something else that you identify with that you wished you hadn't adopted. Beliefs that you didn't choose yourself can damage your self-image.

Another sign that you're not using the past constructively is that a single negative experience is affecting your belief system today. Although these experiences most likely occur in early childhood, they are not limited to that time period. These experiences could bring on erroneous conclusions.

Self-Concept and Self-Belief

When I was in grade school, my teacher changed my self-concept, which in turn changed the direction of the next thirty-plus years of my life. One day in class, we had an assignment to write a small essay on what we wanted to be and why. As she walked around the room, I remember feeling anxious and needing her approval regarding what I had chosen. She stood behind me and said, "Maybe you should consider being a nurse assistant [not even a nurse]. You can't write or read that well, nor add, so you should stay away from journalism, anything analytical … You can still help people, but maybe you should go to trade school."

I didn't know what a trade school was or what analytical meant, but I felt embarrassed, rejected, and disappointed. By the way, my paper said that I wanted to be a child psychiatrist. In addition, I didn't put it on my paper, but in my heart I wanted to run my own practice. I knew that involved running a business because my mother told me so. My teacher's belief about me was an erroneous one, and it was now transferred to my belief. I started to believe I wasn't good enough or smart enough. These beliefs were very limiting and began to affect every part of my life.

Self-belief is crucial to our confidence in our decisions. Our self-concept is formed by our environment, the people we respect, our family, and even the media. Whether we believe our perspective of our self-concept is true or false is determined by our belief system. For example, I believed strongly that the seed my teacher planted (not good enough) was true, along with things everyone else said that watered that seed and all other seeds connected to it. The stronger that belief grew, the more my perception and evaluation of self was affected. It took more than twenty years for me to start changing that self-belief. That initially was the only step that would change my self-concept. Change the self-belief and you will change the self-concept.

Although they were a negative influence in my life, I had an innate resilience that screamed, *I am going to show her and the world that I am enough and I can go to college and succeed.* I later found out that I had dyslexia. That explained so much to me. I got help, studied very hard, worked with tutors and study groups—the works—and eventually received my MBA. But looking back, my reason for wanting so badly to get it was to prove to Ms. D that I could be analytical.

A couple of years later, I was going through another health scare and those feelings of feeling not good enough reemerged. My employer knew I was sick, and it resulted in me not receiving a promotion because I was not able to travel the amount of time that was needed. Feeling rejected and hearing Ms. D's voice, I enrolled in another master's program to prove I was enough whether I received the promotion or not.

Years later, my book was released and many people started to contact me to schedule speaking engagements. Although I was honored to speak at many events, some were looking for someone who held a doctorate. I was also turned down for some TV shows because of the same thing. What do you think happened? Ms. D's voice surfaced, "You're not good enough," so I entered a doctorate program. When I received my doctorate, I realized that Ms. D had influenced many of my life decisions, all because I had given her the power to dictate that I wasn't good enough. It was time for a paradigm shift simply because I realized that not only had Ms. D affected my self-concept for years, but I had also allowed others to do the same thing. I wrote down every negative thought I could think of from my past and asked myself whether the source was credible. Once I answered this, I attempted to turn every thought around into something positive. Here's an example:

> Statement: I'm not good enough.
> Source: Ms. D
> Credible: No.
> Why: Because no one can tell you what you can and can't achieve in second grade or ever. You can achieve anything you want to achieve. I am the evidence of that.
> Restatement: I am more than enough.

Say your restatement every time the negative feeling comes up, and you will begin to believe it and live it daily. Convince yourself that your new belief is possible by using positive experiences that support the new, healthy belief. You can recall past experiences that support the positive belief, or you can create new experiences that you know will support it.

Tips to Build a Positive Self-Belief and Self-Concept

- Remember self-belief is learnable.
- Be aware of the inner negative voice.
- Flip a weakness into a strength.
- Develop your inner "superpowers." You have them!
- Be your own motivational coach, but please reach out for help on your journey. I am so thankful for my mentors and coaches.
- Celebrate the small wins as well as the big ones.
- Create a powerful vision of yourself. Keep on dreaming.

Self-Acceptance

Once you let go of past mistakes and accept yourself, only then can you move forward. After I reframed my negative beliefs, the hardest thing was not constantly mixing what I had felt in the past with what I felt and who I was in the present. After deep reflection, I realized I hadn't let go of the regret, shame, and guilt tied to present decisions that were based on my false self-concept. Because I didn't feel like I was good enough and had accepted that narrative throughout my life, I made mistakes that caused me to feel regret, resentment, shame, and guilt. I realized that I had to forgive myself before I could forgive anyone else.

I read a book by Iyanla Vanzant called *21 Days to Forgiveness*, and it changed my entire perspective on forgiveness. It opened me up and motivated me daily to tell my truth by any means necessary. I found myself waking up every morning and running toward the truth I used to run from. There were times when the negative beliefs paralyzed me, but as I started to feel, I was no longer paralyzed by the beliefs that were nothing but lies.

I had to figure out what I did and didn't do and what I did and didn't feel. Once I figured that out, I was in the room with clarity. I held myself accountable for the things that were easier to hide or blame on someone or a situation. I had to consider how my mistakes affected others. I had to realize that the negative influencers I had trusted and loved had spoken things over my life that just weren't true.

Once I was ready to truly surrender to forgiveness, I set up conversations with the people with whom I wanted to nurture relationships, and I was prepared to hear their feedback regarding my mistakes and theirs. For the others I needed to forgive but not be in relationships with, I went through the steps of forgiving and letting go. Keeping my mind in alignment with this was a process, and it's personal for everyone. Some conversations were very tough, and some took several takes to move forward, but I didn't give up. Those several takes consisted of much communication about our feelings, health, and conflicts, as well as some tears. I took the necessary time to reflect and heal between takes, but I didn't give up.

Love Who You Are through Exercising Self-Love

Embrace your individuality and realize what makes you unique. Until you embrace everything about yourself, good or bad, you will not be able to love yourself. Therefore, you can't take the very first self vow or be truly authentic. There are so many special traits about yourself that are amazing, and the world needs them. Before anyone can embrace you, you have to open your arms to who you are.

Think deeply about who you are and how you would describe yourself to other people. What words would you use? Another useful exercise is to ask four friends who have known you well and whose feedback you trust how they would describe you. Ask them to provide both pros and cons. These exercises can be the most eye-opening experience. You will find out how much you value yourself and if you truly think that you are worthy. Write down what strategy you will use to resolve your biggest struggles. Know that you can overcome anything and it is worth taking your issues one step at a time. You are worth it!

Is it possible to be truly authentic without self-love? The answer is yes. You can be authentically a jerk and obviously lack self-love. It's important to practice self-love because who we become authentically will be a beautiful marriage with self. Self-love, in my experience and quest to define and understand it, is an unconditional feeling of love, appreciation, and acceptance for yourself. Let's define unconditional. It means that no matter what you do, you always love yourself with the same strength. Self-love grows from actions that mature our thoughts and behavior. It also supports who we are physically, psychological, and spiritually.

Creating positive self-love is essential in picking a mate who will enhance who you are and add to your happy lifestyle. A lack of self-love will result in unhealthy choices in who you pick to date or, more importantly, take as your life partner.

Self-love is a process. Trust me. I have been on this journey for years now, and guess what? There is always something new to learn and understand from a deeper sense of intimacy. Evolution confirms that as the layers are peeled back, growth continues. The process is not a destination. Self-love requires you to spend time with self and to disconnect from distractions (e.g., social media, which we will discuss later). I challenge you to carve out at least an hour a day to spend time with you without distractions—no phones, no technology, no people, no tasks. Just you. There is no experience like it.

Tips for Positive Self-Love

- Wake up, look in the mirror, and take three minutes in silence to just be.
- Create positive affirmations for the day, week, or month.
- Encourage yourself when someone is mean to you.
- Respond and don't react. There's a difference.
- Eat food that is healthy for your body.
- Exercise and stretch your body daily.
- Be your first priority. Don't put yourself at the end of the line daily.
- Know that mistakes are only *mis-takes*. Through our mistakes, we often miss the lessons and the gifts through our error. We focus on the error rather than the beauty of what we learned.
- Take yourself out to dinner, to a movie, or on a fabulous date.
- Be honest.
- Be intentional.
- Cry when you need to. Grieve when you need to, too.
- Give yourself permission to rest.

I went through this process, and it took years to truly love myself. Afterward, I realized that the things I didn't like or feel at peace with were learned behaviors from people I respected. I knew these traits weren't the truth of who I was because I had no peace with them. At my core, I felt my truth was the opposite of these traits. I now know that this was my authenticity. I knew who I truly was, whether good or challenging, and it was easier to embrace because I had made the decision to surrender to truth. I had to strategize on how I was going to disconnect from the lies that convinced me it was my truth. I used a four-step strategy: acknowledgement, forgiveness, embracing self-acceptance, and loving self. I had to celebrate my quirky side, the things that may seem weird to some but are what make me, *me.*

People will respect your truth. They will appreciate that authenticity about you. You will begin to attract others who have the same willingness to tell the truth and be authentic. Boost your confidence and develop skills. Turn down the volume of distractions and turn up the clarity. Broaden your experiences. Trust and believe in yourself. Learn to avoid seeking approval. And, finally, take note of your behavior.

When you accept and get comfortable with yourself, you'll learn how to show yourself to the world. Once you show up confident in who you are, you will have a chance to create a compelling and exciting future. Have you ever felt like you were acting the opposite of your true self? I felt like that for most of my life. I can remember traces of this feeling from kindergarten, but early grade school was when I truly felt isolated. When Ms. D made her statement that day, shortly after she put me in remedial reading. I knew I was not who she was saying I was. At the same time, my voice was silenced and I lost the courage to speak up for myself. Deep within, something was telling me that something was different about me or maybe that I just saw things differently than others.

I remember another teacher in grade school, Mr. A, would say, "It doesn't say that on the board." It was so frustrating because it truly did say what I was reading with my eyes. Wouldn't it have been great if I'd had the right title of dyslexic instead of being thought dumb or accused of not paying attention? I think my teachers felt that, and I began to believe it. During those years, I wasn't choosing to hide myself, but in my high school years, I remember making the choice to be more of what was accepted, even if that meant swallowing my voice more and more. As I grew older, my voice seemed to leave. I could see the results of not sharing my voice in all of my relationships, including with friends, my family, and boyfriends.

Narcissism versus Self-Love

Many people debate whether narcissistic behavior and self-love are one in the same. Self-love is the ability to extend kindness and compassion to yourself. It is also the ability to consistently have healthy conflict. Self-love is unapologetic about being honest, having healthy intentions, and making healthy choices. Narcissists, on the other hand, live in a fantasy, the opposite of honesty and a true sense of reality.

Self-love goes hand in hand with being authentic, but a narcissist is most comfortable in the fake self. When we are authentic, we embrace all that we are. A narcissist considers him- or herself to be of greater value than others, believing he or she is entitled to the best of everything. Narcissistic personality disorder should not be confused with healthy self-esteem or self-love. Self-love is when you give yourself positive affirmations, boundaries, and forgiveness daily. Narcissists, on the other hand, lack a healthy sense of self-love and will work themselves to the bone for external validation while actively dismissing anyone and anything that gets in the way of achieving their desired reward.

A narcissist is an unfulfilled person. Narcissism hollows you out, but self-love fills you up. A narcissist is greedy and self-absorbed and has no feelings of empathy, but self-love is quite aware that you need to feel to heal. Self-love allows you to more deeply connect through exercising intimacy with self and others. If we can't appreciate our depth of courage, power, beauty, as well as our flaws, we won't be able to see and appreciate that in others. Self-love fosters emotional, psychological, and physical health. Loving yourself means getting to the internal core of your human existence and finding that sweet spot where you can be yourself and be happy with who you are.

Having healthy self-love and self-esteem means knowing that we have a number of strengths and positive qualities, but it also means knowing that our weaknesses are opportunities to grow. If we are not secure or if we have a major challenge with loving self, we tend to compare ourselves to others. Remember the only expert that you are obligated to be is the expert on you.

A narcissist is convinced that others are less than what he or she is. Narcissists are characterized by arrogance, entitlement, exhibitionism, and the praise from others, and they feel that they are superior to others. A narcissist plays the role of a friend, a committed partner, a good employer instead of actually performing the actions of that role. When you take responsibility of self-love and have a strong self-commitment, you want to extend that to others. Narcissists, however, don't have much incentive to do a thorough job or take responsibility when things go wrong.

Now that we are clear on what narcissism and self-esteem are, let's talk about when they start. Both narcissism and self-esteem start to develop around the age of seven. At this age, children draw heavily on social comparisons with others and start to evaluate themselves along the lines of "I am a loser" or "I am worthy" or "I am special." Children come to view themselves as they perceive they are seen by others.[2]

"The development of self-esteem and narcissism are also influenced by different parenting styles. Narcissism tends to develop in tandem with parental overvaluation. Parents who raise children who exhibit high levels of narcissism tend to overclaim their child's knowledge (e.g., 'My child knows everything there is to know about math'), overestimate their child's IQ, overpraise their child's performance, and even tend to give their child a unique name to help him or her stand out from the crowd. Eventually, the child internalizes these self-views, and they unconsciously drive the child's interactions with others."[3]

---

[2] Scott Barry Kaufman, "Narcissism and Self-Esteem Are Very Different," *Beautiful Minds* (blog), *Scientific American*, October 29, 2017, https://blogs.scientificamerican.com/beautiful-minds/narcissism-and-self-esteem-are-very-different/.

[3] Kaufman, "Narcissism."

"In contrast, high self-esteem develops in tandem with parental warmth. Parents who raise children who exhibit high levels of self-esteem tend to treat their children with affection, appreciation, and fondness. They treat their children as though they matter. Eventually, this parenting practice leads to the children internalizing the message that they are worthy individuals, a core aspect of healthy self-esteem."[4]

Ten Signs of a Narcissist

- always talks about himself or herself
- tends to fantasize
- believes he or she is superior
- requires constant praise
- exhibits a sense of entitlement
- takes advantage of others
- is often envious of others
- enjoys being the center of attention
- lacks empathy
- possesses boundless ambition

To be authentic in a healthy and positive way, you must have self-love and if you have identified yourself as a narcissist or the people around you have narcissistic behavior, you must break up from that relationship even if it means breaking up from the toxic part of you. If you desire to be authentic and evolve within that authenticity, being a narcissist or tolerating one puts a major separation between you and your authentic self.

Purpose through Living Authentically

Once I committed to unleashing the true me under all the layers of pain, hurt, rejection, disappointment, and other negative feelings, Michelle R. Hannah showed up, and I really started to like her. Indeed, I started to fall in love with her. To get there, I had to choose to share my real life no matter who didn't like it. I had to practice mindfulness daily and be intentional about my actions. (Mindfulness is the psychological process of bringing one's attention to experiences occurring in the present moment, which one can develop through the practice of meditation and through other training.) I had to make sure I had the right intentions. I had to give myself time and be kind to myself.

---

[4] Kaufman, "Narcissism."

I realized that for twenty years I did what I had to do until I could do what I wanted to do. What I wanted to do was my purpose for existing. I realized that the greatest wound was being rejected for being my authentic self. I needed to reconnect to the self that took my first breath into this world. I had to nurture myself along the way. I had to learn to stay mindful about separating my own thoughts from those of someone else. I had to choose a route that worked in alignment with how I really felt. I was more confident when I was authentic with others instead of being disingenuous with what I really felt.

Once you are comfortable and confident with who you are, the clarity that comes is like the feeling of relief after labor. Seeing that baby for the first time is a love I still can't find the words to describe. Once you unleash your purpose, the feeling is very similar. Purpose is why you were born; it's the manifestation of your existence. Just be yourself, all of you. When you are authentic, it feels so good and free, specifically with people you trust. Being authentic is natural; you simply can't fake what's real. Know that a powerful legacy is based on how many lives you touch.

Self Vows Questions

Authenticity

1. Am I living my truth or someone else's? If so, what are the consequences of betraying my own truth?
   Love note: Answering this question will be challenging if you are unsure about your own truth. Also, you might not be betraying all aspects of your truth. Perhaps you have given in to being unhappy in one area. Although it's just one area, there is still a part of you that is living a lie.

2. Am I enjoying my life? What are the reasons for my enjoyment?
   Love note: Truly living is enjoying life regardless of the challenges that come along with it.

3. Am I surviving or living?
   Love note: Surviving feels like dragging one foot in front of the other. Living feels like you are doing exactly what you want to be doing. It feels joyful and peaceful.

4. Am I doing what I want to do in life, or is my own fear holding me back?
   Love note: Doing what you love is so fulfilling and the epitome of freedom. If you're not doing it or at least taking steps to do whatever the *it* is, then you know

fear may be at the core of it. Remember we explored about barriers? This is a good example.

5. What is my purpose? How have I unleashed it to share with the world?
   Love note: Purpose isn't easy to unleash and can be equally challenging to identify, but once you do, the next step is to unleash it to the world. The world truly needs to experience why you're here and why you exist.

6. How do I describe my self-concept? How does it affect my decisions?
   Love note: Self-concept truly affects our decisions and can determine whether a decision is healthy or unhealthy. Reflect on where your self-concept comes from.

Get Ready to Do Your Work!

Authenticity is a tough journey, but it is one of the most courageous steps you will ever take. I haven't met anyone who doesn't want to be free, but many don't want to do the work. I have heard many clients say that they're not happy, but they are content with unhappiness. Of course this logically doesn't make sense, but it does when you are unhealthy and used to being paralyzed and in pain that comes from living a lie. I have realized that when people acknowledge that they are living in the image and are ready to feel, all they need are steps and guidance to reclaim their freedom. If you're ready, let me give you some tips and a few exercises before you move to the next chapter.

Tips to Build a Strong Self-Concept

- Accept what is, but be confident that you can change your choices.
- Be observant of your breath. It will make a difference in your perspective on reality.
- Daily meditation will help you to be clear about your own thoughts.
- Let go of anything that causes you to feel the opposite of self-love.

Exercise 1: Daily Affirmations

Perform the following steps to connect to transforming affirmations daily.

1. Check your breathing. Is it slow, fast, shallow, deep, or irregular? The answer will reveal to you any underlying fear, pain, or unresolved issues.

- Breathing slow and deep can calm the nervous system.
- Fast breathing can suggest anxiety.
- Shallow breathing can suggest stress.
- Deep breathing suggests relaxation.
- Irregular breathing suggests anxiety.

2. Meditate on a specific topic that is challenging for you (e.g., self-love).
3. Surrender to what God has for you and put your hand in your bowl of written affirmations. The affirmation you choose will be just for you.
4. Recite the affirmation throughout the day until it feels true. For example: I accept and have everything about myself.

Exercise 2: Scripting

Scripting is being very intentional and exact about how you want your life to be. In addition, it's focused on how to manifest those things into your life. In my opinion, it's necessary to focus on both. If we beg and show up desperate and expecting a shift in our finances, relationships, or emotional and spiritual life with no shift in the way we think, we are mistaken. Whatever you put out into the universe is what will show up. If you continue to complain about being broke, alone, and unhappy, what do you think you will receive? You get more and more of what you put out. Isn't that enough to change your thinking? Be aware that the ego will attempt to convince you that you are lying when you script, but ignore it. You are confessing how you want life to be and manifesting it.

The following questions will help you with scripting. Love note: Starting your scripting statements with "I am," "I know," and "I have" will speak to the present and send the energy into the universe that suggests it has already happened.

1. What is the perfect career for you?
   Sample scripting statement: I have a great career as a TV host.

2. Where would you live while doing what you love?
   Sample scripting statement: I am bicoastal and living in New York City and California.

3. What's the greatest feeling in the morning you want to feel? What do you want to taste? What do you want to see?
   Sample scripting statement: I am at peace every morning while drinking my Chai tea. I see the ocean and beautiful city buildings while the sun comes up.

4. What products, programs, and services will I focus on to accomplish my financial goals?
   Sample scripting statement: I have sold ten programs, have five new coaching clients, and have sold twenty thousand books.

5. How will I market all of this for the next ninety days?
   Sample scripting statement: My social media is increasing in followers, likes, and customers thanks to my new products.

6. What kind of living environment do you want?
   Sample scripting statement: I have a three-bedroom condo that is spacious, with neutral colors and accented with a pop of bright colors. I have large windows that make it feel as though I am inside and outside at the same time. I live on the nineteenth floor, and no buildings or trees block my beautiful view of the ocean and city.

7. How much money do I want to make?
   Sample scripting statement: I make $750,000 a year. It feels so good to wake up and know all my bills are paid, I have no debt, and I have more than enough to travel, buy my daughter a house, and retire my mother.

8. What is healthy ideally for you?
   Sample scripting statement: I am pain free and at my ideal weight.

9. What do you want to have as your daily diet?
   Sample scripting statement: I have vegetables daily, and I am dairy free.

Remember your feelings and the vibrations in which you operate determine what you are going to get back from the universe in the future. We are creating our future through the thoughts, actions, and energy that we experiencing now!

Reflective Notes

Reflective Notes

Reflective Notes

CHAPTER 3

For Better, For Worse

Accept that you will experience many situations in life. Some situations are beyond your control, while others are determined by the choices you make. That is why it is so important to be fully present as you live your life. Being fully present means having your focus, attention, thoughts, and feelings all fixed on the task at hand. If you are speaking to somebody, then your attention and energy are focused on that person and what he or she is saying.

In this climate of technology, being fully present is difficult because we are taught that if we are good at multitasking, then we are mastering being able to accomplish many things in a short period of time or at the same time. But think about it: What sense does that make? Why not be focused on one thing and master that?

Before you enter a lifelong commitment, it is crucial to be aware of your decisions, to be able to articulate your feelings, and to able to reflect on why you feel and react in certain ways. Even if you contract a debilitating disease, you'll know that you are strong. You will never abandon yourself, because every feeling and every experience you have stays with you. If you have just achieved your greatest accomplishment and no one seems to be cheering you on—or even noticing—know that you are your greatest cheerleader. Be there and be gentle with yourself for better or for worse.

Clarissa's Story

I have learned to commit to "for better, for worse" with a forgiving and joyful attitude. At seventy-one years old, life has taught me that the more you fight against the process, the more you will manifest the worst into your circumstance. Relaxing and reflecting in the process causes you to see the lesson clearly. There's nothing better than clarity other than the willingness to forgive and stay joyful no matter the challenge. A smile may not resolve pain, but it makes your overall outlook better.

My biological father was not active in my life until adulthood. It was the worst feeling growing up two blocks away from him and having no relationship. I remember wanting a dress from Macy's, and he made up an excuse as to why he didn't get it. Shortly after, I saw him in a grocery store, and we didn't speak; it was as if we were not who we were to each other. It's funny to look back at that and realize that he created an environment that was the opposite of authenticity from the very beginning. Seeing my father in the store and asking him for help to get the dress, after all, the dress ,in my opinion was the least he could do. Needless to say, he didn't. I was angry and bewildered.

I was determined that I would never ask him for anything again. I felt that if I could pick cotton to go to the county fair, I could find a way to buy my own dress. That "I will show you" attitude and anger poured into other relationships in my life. Before my father passed, we were at least to a point of forgiveness. It's sad that he was emotionally unavailable, but I realized I also married an emotionally unavailable person. Interesting how we marry sometimes the worst part of our fathers.

My late husband was a wonderful provider and very stable. He never missed work. However, he didn't have the capacity to fill the emotional intimacy cup. I was so determined to marry stability, I neglected to ensure that he was emotionally available. He didn't know how to be, and I found that the anger that existed toward my father spilled out into my marriage because I married the thing that I missed. My father didn't fill the hole that he created, so it just expanded through the years.

I have seen the generational pathology of this in my daughter and granddaughter. We all have suffered from that attitude: "I don't need anyone. I'll get it for myself." Because I made the decision to choose the attitude of anger and pain instead of forgiveness and joy, many of my obstacles became worse or I stayed trapped in the feeling of being stuck. My worst fear is that my granddaughter will feel the way I did regarding my father and the way my child felt going through the pain of divorce.

It's funny how we end up willing closer the things we fear the most. My daughter went through a divorce, and my granddaughter grew up without her father. Although painful, it didn't kill us, but it did make us stronger. My daughter, Dr. Michelle R. Hannah, is the author of this book, and my granddaughter is a recent double major graduate of a prestigious university. I realize that our purpose was the result of our individual pain. I realize that I had the mind-set to commit for better or for worse, but along my journey, I didn't have the tools to get through the process in a healthy way.

My worst was to be poor or to lose what I had. Well, the worst happened. I lost my husband to a heart attack, lost my house to a short sale, and lost my best friend within a forty-eight month timeframe. I stayed in the pain of the worst for twenty years after the fact. Again, I was committed to not give up, but I wasn't committed to the process. When you complain, live in fear, or don't invest in yourself, whether emotionally, physically, or spiritually, you sabotage the feeling of better within your worst or the better that forms in the breakthrough. You have to lean into the break before the breakthrough.

Now my better is defined very differently than a car, home, or designer clothes. It's creating generational wealth and investing in myself and in others. My better is defined by knowing that love is all there is. It's being able to see my kids love one another. It's my granddaughter graduating from college and my daughter being emotionally and physically healed. It's peace. I have realized that our foundation determines the capacity of much better, and our attitude, forgiveness, and joyful outlook determine our worst.

Now I stand at seventy-one, taking the self vows I wish I would have taken forty-six years ago when I was having my first child. I would have passed those seven vows on to my daughter and read to her that story instead of fairytales. However, my life has built character and ushered me along the road of nonjudgment, peace, and forgiveness, and as I broaden my capacity of love, it deepens how I give it. I am committed for better or for worse to live the vows for as long as I shall live. Funnily enough, I gave my daughter life and love, and she in turn gave me life through the seven vows that changed my life.

Author's Note

It's been some time now since my mom took the self vows, and when I say it's been a whirlwind, I truly mean it. It's brought so many beautiful blessings, but I'd like to share one in particular with you. After three years of a gentleman's consistent pursuit of my mom, she surrendered to love. I witnessed how this man looks at my mom, treats her like the truly phenomenal lady she is, and wants to spend the rest of his life with her. He just wants her to be happy. She so deserves it. It doesn't take away from my dad, but as she evolved, God prepared him for her. His intention, of course, is to take the vows and extend them to my mom until he takes his last breath. Of course, no one knows the future, but I'm just glad that I am still here to witness what I prayed about for at least fifteen years. Marriage is not always the bottom line. Sometimes it's just finding someone to love you and be your companion through this thing we call life.

The self vows can be contagious if your heart is open, and as God would have it, her companion, who is eighty-one, took his self vows. You are never too old. Thank you, Father God, for the manifestation of love. You can absolutely find love at seventy-one. Take the self vows!

Self Vows Questions

Evolve

1. Am I willing to evolve even if my friends, family, or mate are not?
   Love note: Everyone grows at his or her own capacity and rate, but if your friends, family, or mate are not willing to evolve or are evolving at a much slower pace, distance may be needed if it affects your growth.

2. Do I lift myself up when I improve, or do I consistently complain when something isn't exactly the way I want it? Explain.

3. What are affirmations that I use daily that result in the positive relationship I have with self?
   Love note: Affirmations are great, but they are effective when they are intentional.

4. What is the best thing about my relationship with self?
   Love note: Learning self is such an interesting journey. Just when you think you have mastered it, life happens and you evolve in ways you never thought you could. Next the reintroduction of self happens again.

The Worst

1. Am I willing to go through the worst thing I can imagine and still stay committed to myself? What would that worst thing be, and how would I handle it?
   Love note: The worst things that can happen in life teach us great lessons about self and others.

2. What is the worst thing about facing my true self? What is the best thing about facing my true self?
   Love note: Facing the truth can be scary, but it is always the best thing about who we are. Truth is freedom, and freedom is peace

Forgiveness

1. Am I willing to forgive myself for everything?
   Love note: Forgiveness is a gift you give to yourself and others.

2. When I am irritable and tired, do I lash out at others? If not, how do I take care of myself when I'm feeling that way?
   Love note: Being compassionate to yourself when you are irritated is crucial because when you bring calm to self, you will have no energy to lash out at self or others.

Tab's Story

When I meditate on the self vow of "for better, for worse," it suggests that through the ups and the downs, I'm here for it all. I took this vow two years ago with my husband, and I can't say that I truly realized the gravity of the vow until my marriage started to go through some challenges. I was faced with the decision of whether I would stay committed to this vow. We decided to seek out help, and that resulted in us meeting Dr. Michelle. After several sessions, she realized that it was very important for us to define what the vows meant to self. This was a concept that I had never heard of or thought about.

A couple of months later, I attended the Self Vows Retreat, and by the second day, I was thinking deeply about those particular vows and how they related to my life. I asked myself what "for better, for worse" meant to me regarding self.

A story came to mind. I was twenty-eight years old and had been living on my own for nearly a year, and I loved it! Just one month shy of my first year of moving out, my transmission went out in my car. I was devastated. Not only did I not have backup transportation, but I definitely didn't have $3,000 for a new transmission. I could barely afford my bills as it was! With a broken transmission and a car that I was still paying for, my options were limited. I had to humble myself and ask my family for help. I realized I had to move back home. Living with a close family member again, totally broke, and with no car, I instantly felt like a loser. The negative self-talk did not help in what I felt was a terrible situation. For me, the worst was having to depend on my family again at age twenty-eight. Once I left my family's home, I was committed to never going back. I was embarrassed with myself. This was the lowest I had been in all my adult years.

My first night back at my family's house, I cried to myself and prayed for God to show me how I was going to get through this. Later that week, a family member agreed to let me borrow money to get a new car. He had me make a budget and stick to it. I had to humble myself again and realize I couldn't afford to live on my own without a second job. I made the decision to get a part-time job. I had never been so exhausted in my life. But all my hard work eventually paid off. Months later, I had paid the family member back and was able to live on my own once again, but this time I stayed out and never put myself in a financial situation like that again.

I realized that there was no need to be embarrassed about the situation because it was a lesson for me from a financial point of view, and it helped me make the choice to disconnect from pride. Dr. Michelle shared with me that the greatest leaders show their *woundedness* and ask for help. I thought to myself that if great leaders feel this way, then who am I to feel embarrassed about asking for help?

Since the Self Vows Retreat, I have learned to implement all the vows in my life and in my marriage. Having that foundation gave me the courage to start my own business and connect to "for richer, for poorer." No matter what, I am committed to my business, dreams, and goals. I must say that I am proud of myself because I asked for help and my support team rose up and met me. As a result, I have completed six events in three months. Who am I? I am Tabs the creative, event stylist. I am a loving daughter, wife, sister, friend and phenomenal woman. Yes, that's me.

I committed to fostering the better part of myself, consistently encouraging myself with weekly affirmations. I committed to making most decisions from an objective point of view.

I realized that this vow meant that whether I got myself into trouble, felt hurt, sad, or sick, or didn't feel good about myself physically, mentally, or spiritually, I could focus on the best of myself under any circumstances. I promised myself to keep moving forward, growing, learning, and being the best woman I can be.

Most importantly, I know I can show up differently in my marriage for better or for worse because I took the vow to self and now can share it with my husband.

For Better For Worst

Yolanda's story: Yolanda is my best friend. I have had the privilege of knowing her for 35 plus years. We weren't always connected but even in our separation the love never left. Funny how time and growth deepens your love. Yolanda lost her mom at 27 and at that time her relationship with her father was strained. Yolanda was 1 of 3 girls. Her relationship with her mother was important and so needed at this point of her life. A couple of years later she met her husband, but not having her mom in attendance due to her death was a bittersweet moment. Yolanda's desire to have a child was another disappointment due to an unknown condition. The next blow she was dealt was being told she had breast cancer. She had to take chemo for a year and is presently still on meds that cause various side effects. Although her husband has been her rock; 17 years later she had to pull from her authentic self to rise up and be her own advocate, cheerleader, mother, best friend, spiritual advisor and the depth of love that can only come from self. I truly believe this is why Yolanda's marriage has lasted so long because she was able to have her back for better or for worse no matter what. By giving that gift to herself, she was able to give that same commitment to her husband, friends and family. I'm sure by showing her husband her strength; it provided him with the strength to be there for her even more.

Yolanda and I had a long separation that I take most of the responsibility for. I was going through a challenging time in my life that left me isolated and extremely depressed. While she was about to get married, I was about to go through a divorce. I needed her so much, but I couldn't rain on her happiness. I felt like a failure and just took the coward's way out and ran to isolate. I didn't trust that she could handle being my friend and not compromise her newfound happiness. I had done the opposite. I didn't stay committed to self, and I was desperately trying to abandon everything about me. I was in the abyss. This lasted for the next several years and then I moved and lost contact with all of our mutual friends.

Years had passed; I had survived carcinoma insitu of the cervix, raising my daughter as a single parent, and was surrounded by breast cancer survivors that I was assisting through my foundation CLF. For some reason Yolanda was on my mind and in my dreams. A year later I moved back to Los Angeles, CA

Although I was closing the doors to my foundation, I continued to attract breast cancer survivors. I could literally be walking down the street and a stranger would start speaking to me about their battle with breast cancer and how their friendships helped them through their journey. Never would I have ever imagined that shortly after I would get Yolanda's contact info and my hope was that we would be reunited. We were reunited but sadly I was informed she had breast cancer and was about to fight one of the biggest fights of her life. Who was I to just enter back into her life after all these years and expect her to accept my help? Perhaps she had a new best friend that had taken my place. I reached out but she wasn't ready to talk to me or see me, but she did say I could send her cards or leave some gifts of encouragement on her doorstep. I wanted to run because I felt rejected, but not this time. For better or for worse, I was going to be there even if it was from a distance. Through witnessing Yolanda's commitment to self it made me want to fight harder for my own medical condition. I was in excruciating pain, but as she lost her hair, weight and taste buds, her spirit was strong and a testament of for better for worse, I still love myself. That love spilled over for the world to see. Although

I have always been a giver, I have many times neglected myself. She is a giver as well, but while she was going through her treatment I observed what it is to give to self and take care of your needs first. You see, I wanted to see her everyday if I could, but that wasn't the best thing for her. I had to respect that and trust that she would take care of herself.

For practically a year, I stayed my distance physically, but emotionally I was right there holding her hand. We were finally physically reunited and she was cancer free. I realized in that moment that the dreams I had of her and all the random breast cancer survivors that I bumped into on the street, that had shared their survivor stories with me were all a part of preparing me for the journey that Yolanda and I would take, for better or for worse. When reunited with each other, I realized after 5 minutes it was as if we had never been separated for 17 years. True love and friendship can heal any pain and offense; we just have to be willing to surrender to the journey.

Take a moment and think of the worst thing that could happen to you. Take a deep breath and reflect on what would be your 1st step. Would it be to run, to sink into self-doubt, and negative self-talk, thus betraying yourself? If you answered yes to any of those questions, you have not taken the Self Vow for better or for worse. If you can't take that vow to self, you will have a huge challenge demonstrating that to another. Take a moment and write down all the things that could happen that would make you run or betray yourself. Ask yourself: what's the difference between the you that goes through the best of times and the you that is going through the worst of times. When you are living authentically the only thing that should change between the two is that your commitment is stronger and grows deeper. When you start to live a lie when you are in the worst of times in an effort to protect self or prevent disappointment, you only make it worse. With such a negative reaction, with every breath you are deciding to betray yourself.

On the other hand, if you rise to the occasion each and every time challenging things happen or if the worst happens, you are ready to take the self vow and teach others how it looks and feels to live this vow.

Get Ready to Do Your Work

When you engage in negative self-talk, your tone is usually not compassionate. You are not being kind to yourself. In crisis, a challenging day or situation is when we need to be gentle and encouraging with ourselves—mind, body, and soul. How can we extend ourselves in a loving way to others but fail at self-care? When you make up your mind to be committed to self, communication in the worst of times is essential to get through the day. I speak to myself throughout the day. Sometimes it's through action and other times it's through encouragement or affirmations. Think about it. When you speak to others in a less than loving way, the results can be hurt feelings, misunderstandings, or worse, shutting down. I have found that love and a soft tone sets the direction of any conversation. With that said, start with a gentle tone with yourself, and you will be on a healthy path.

Tips to Cure Negative Self-Talk

- Acknowledge negative thoughts.
- Reflect on the evidence to support or not support your thoughts.
- Reframe your thoughts.
- Ask yourself what's the worst thing that could happen if your thoughts were true.
- Replace the negative talk and reaffirm the truth.

Exercise: Feeling or Fact, True or False?

When we are going through the worst of times, it is very hard to stay positive. We tend to accept the worst of the situation as being the truth for the rest of our lives instead of just for the moment. We will listen more easily to others who fuel the negativity rather than those who focus on the positive. Those who tell us, no matter how dark it looks, to have faith and keep going, we ignore once we are in a dark place. I have the perfect solution for that this exercise. Remember some things we feel about ourselves or our situations are not always facts but rather feelings. Once we realize the difference, know that we can change a feeling and, at times, even a fact, depending on our resilience.

1. Get a piece of paper and fold it in half.
2. Write on one side everything you think is a feeling and on the other side everything you think is a fact.
3. Once you have completed it, go through the list and place a FE by each item to confirm it's a feeling and an FA to confirm it's fact.
4. Determine if you have more facts that are negative than feelings or vice versa.
5. Decide to change the negative feelings by infusing them with affirmations, positive advice, and positive actions. This will change the trajectory of the negative feelings into more positive ones.
6. The facts are the facts, so accept them. However, just because you accept a fact doesn't mean that you don't have the power to change it. Sometimes you can't change the situation, but you can change you.

Reflective Notes

Reflective Notes

Reflective Notes

CHAPTER 4

For Richer, for Poorer

Sometimes the messages about prosperity that we get from our family of origin are far from our own truth. If your parents were poor or middle-class and they taught you that you can only go so far, you do not have to accept their truth. You don't have to maintain a poverty state of mind. Your openness and independence might scare or threaten some people because your truth exposes their falsehood. For example, I have heard people say to their family members, "You are black and a woman, and you will never be as successful as ..." To the contrary, any human being who believes that he or she can do anything through God, from whom all strength comes, can succeed. You might have to face the fear that has kept you in a poverty state of mind. And the choices you make might force your family members to acknowledge that some of their beliefs are actually lies perpetuated over multiple generations.

You can choose to be different and to educate yourself. If you seek truth, it will find you. You can break the cycle and teach your kids differently. A rich state of mind is not just financial; it's mental, spiritual, and physical. On the other hand, if you come from a wealthy family (however you define wealthy), it's important that you use your status to help others by teaching them what you know. Never think you're better because someone doesn't have what you have. If you are rich in mind, body, and soul, you will break through even if you lose your money and career. Your resilience will hold you up.

Michelle's Story, told by Michelle R. Hannah

Michelle, my soul sister ... I knew when I met her twenty years ago that she was something special. A sister that is a soul mate is someone who accepts you—all of you. Every woman deserves a *soul sister*. You know you're soul sisters when you can be separated for nineteen years and with one call, it's as if you never stopped talking. As we spoke for hours, I found out that although we were apart, we had gone through the same things almost at the same time, just from different perspectives. Funny how you can be miles away but suffering from some of the same things. As she spoke, I felt sad that I couldn't be there but at the same time happy about where we were presently. We had both written books, traveled as speakers, and were coaches. My book was *The Breaking Point*, and her book was *Spirit Check*—amazing books of self-reflection. Although these two books intersect on several perspectives, they have different approaches to looking within, the steps that are needed to break up with toxicity, surrender to the lessons, face fears and pains, and take the path to unleash your purpose.

Spirit Check focuses on assessing your emotions by a daily check-in. By doing this, you will know if you are operating from a toxic place and whether you are in agreement with that toxicity. Agreeing to toxicity is remaining stuck or not taking the appropriate steps that change the trajectory of our path. Agreeing to allow negative things or people in your sacred space of health and peace offers a home for negative emotions. Once you begin to invest in that negativity, your return will be those negative emotions to manifest physically or through your actions. Your thoughts affect your behavior, so we have to keep our mind in a place of love and peace.

As we spoke, she expressed that she had suffered a heart attack, and the core reason was unresolved issues, toxic situations, the lack of checking in with self, and the challenge of managing stress. It was matters of the heart that manifested through the heart—the organ being affected. I have observed her life and her dedication to her emotional well-being, and the result has been an accountability partner for me, regardless of us not talking every day or seeing each other regularly. It's the evidence of how she lives her life, and that helps me to keep committed to my self vows.

The vow "for richer, for poorer" comes to mind when I think about her journey. Over the years, she allowed people to affect how she felt about herself, her purpose, and the courage to stand in her truth. She had unknowingly agreed to tolerate the negativity that was introduced to her time and time again. Accepting this in her life left her with a poor state of self. Instead of accepting a rich state of self, she had given power to the people who hurt her, and we know that hurt people hurt people. In this case, she hurt herself by giving the people who hurt her power. We allow people to hurt us, but we must not put our ability to heal or exercise overall balance in others' hands. Where there is no balance, there is no stability. If you experience too much anger, it can damage your cardiac health. It is important to strike a balance—to manage your anger and express it in a healthy way so that you don't hurt your arteries and heart.[5]

---

[5] "Emotions and Feelings," Heart and Stroke Foundation, accessed January 3, 2020, https://www.heartandstroke.ca/heart/recovery-and-support/emotions-and-feelings.

Michelle was dealing with anger, depression, and anxiety due to swallowing her pain and dimming her light, and she was disconnected from her voice. She was officially aware, after awaiting heart surgery, that she had been operating with a poor heart literally and figuratively. "It is important to control your worry not just because you will worry less and feel better, but because less worry means less stress for your heart. This applies to the entire range of stressors, from a small episode of acute panic to a larger context such as living through a natural disaster. For all the reasons outlined above, a new emotion-based approach to heart health, called cardiac psychology, is receiving increasing interest."[6]

Michelle realized that she had to treat the mind in order to improve the heart. This awareness prompted her choice to embrace a wealthy mind, heart, and overall emotional well-being. Walking or living in your wealthy place means being more focused on the intangible things, such as peace, love, joy, and patience. Once we choose to focus on those things and check in daily with ourselves, a shift will happen, and we will operate in our higher selves—for richer.

Once you make up your mind to have a prosperous outlook on life, you will begin to connect more and more to the desire to live authentically. Choosing to be authentic has a tendency to motivate you to unleash your purpose and to desire an intimate relationship with a healthy lifestyle, emotionally, physically, and spiritually. She fell in love with self-care and the power of using her voice. Sometimes you have to get your emotions in check so that you have the clarity to get your spirit in check. Our actions don't reflect our wealthy mind-set when we allow our negative thoughts to overpower our greatness.

I realized how important protecting your heart and your mind is through her powerful story of for richer, for poorer. Observing her life and experiencing our special relationship of being soul sisters has not only kept me accountable, but it has required me to do daily spirit checks and, no matter what the situation, never dim my voice.

We will be tested for richer, for poorer in life. Notice there is no "or" because you will experience both in this life. Michelle's experience with for richer, for poorer was learning to strike a balance and never getting stuck again in emotional pain, by managing stress and anger. We are in control of ourselves and not what life might bring to us. Check in with yourself daily in an effort to determine whether you are operating in a poor state of self or a rich state of self. The choice is yours to make the shift.

---

[6] Srini Pillay, "Managing Our Emotions Can Save Your Heart," *Harvard Health Blog*, May 9, 2016, https://www.health.harvard.edu/blog/managing-emotions-can-save-heart-201605099541.

Self Vows Questions—For Richer

Self-Relationship

1. Is your self-relationship wealthy? Why or why not?
   Love note: Intangible forms of wealth are more important than tangible ones.

2. Is your self-relationship profitable? Why is it useful? What are its benefits?
   Love note: In business, it's always best to be profitable, but breaking even for a season is not necessarily a catastrophe if you learn invaluable lessons.

3. What am I investing in myself?
   Love note: Every smart businessperson wants a return on her or his investment. Are you receiving your ROI on self? Remember if you invest good stuff, you get good stuff in return. Be careful what you invest.

Financial Goals

1. Do I have financial goals? What are they? How often and how effectively do I communicate about them?
   Love note: Having goals keeps us accountable. It may be better to just set weekly and quarterly goals so that you are not overwhelmed. Once you accomplish those, then move on to yearly.

2. Is there a legal reason, such as a felony or misdemeanor conviction, that prevents me from pursuing certain types of careers? If so, what are my options?
   Love note: Certain convictions can affect your future goals and determine whether you can achieve them. For example, if you have a felony and your dream is to work for the FBI, it will not be possible. We have all experienced mistakes, so it's important that we have a plan that first forgives self and then identifies healthy options.

3. What do I want to do during retirement? At what age would I like to retire? Do I plan to begin another career after I retire?
   Love note: When we are in our youth, we think retirement is lifetimes away, but then when we reach forty it becomes so much closer, and at sixty if we don't have a plan, we will feel the consequences.

4. How will I approach wills and life insurance?

   Love note: Many people are not prepared to die, but when they do, in addition to the extreme grief, family members have no life insurance or wills to assist afterward. In many circumstances, you can take care of these things online, or with a few calls and perhaps a physical.

Perspective on Money

1. Do I want to be wealthy, or am I only interested in having no stress over paying bills?

   Love note: Wealth creates legacy and generational wealth, something to think about if you are more aligned with just being able to pay your bills.

Employment

1. What if I get relocated because of a job opportunity? How will I handle leaving family, friends, and what is familiar to me?

   Love note: I had to relocate, and it was the most joyful and painful experience of my life. It was a major risk, and it stretched my courage and resilience, but it was one of my best lessons on being "good enough."

Money Decisions

1. What happens most of the time when I want to purchase something that I can't afford? What is the outcome?

   Love note: Spending more than you have is never a good choice, and the result can be a lifetime of problems. Choose wisely.

2. In the next ten years, what will my financial portfolio look like?

   Love note: Plan for the best, but prepare for the worst. A plan is crucial to achieving what you desire.

Marriage

1. I'm scared of the marriage commitment because ... (fill in the blank).

   Love note: If you are scared to commit to self, don't you think that committing to another will be connected and met with that same fear?

2. What is the role of a wife? What is the role of a husband?
   Love note: It's important to respect our family of origin's definition of these roles, but what are your definitions? Consider spiritual definitions of these roles as well.

3. What excites me about exploring my relationship with self? What excites me about marriage?
   Love note: Remember this answer in times of trouble, and don't start to take your beautiful relationship with self or another for granted.

4. Do I follow the philosophy that my money is my money when it comes to a potential spouse?
   Love note: Try the philosophy that there is no yours, only ours.

5. How would I feel about marrying someone with a strong work ethic, or am I comfortable with constantly having to motivate him or her to go to work? If it's the latter, how does that make me feel?
   Love note: Perhaps you plan to one day be married or want to be in a healthy relationship which is why it's important to identify certain characteristics that may be opposite of your values is key.

6. Should I get married now or wait until I am more financially healthy? If I wait, how much have I committed to save, or have I not agreed upon an amount?
   Love note: Beginning a marriage with no debt, a budget, and a year's worth of rent or mortgage payments decreases stress immensely. It's hard enough adjusting to married life; financial pressures on top of that can cause irreparable problems.

7. Who took care of the financial matters of my household while growing up?
   Love note: Whom we learn our financial perspectives from weighs a lot on how we handle our financial portfolios.

Self Vows Questions—For Poorer

Relationship with Debt

1. How do I feel about debt? Do I have any debt? If so, how much?
   Love note: If the environment you grew up in was debt, your relationship with debt might be thinking that it's just a way of life. On the other hand, you may

make an effort at any means necessary to avoid debt at all costs. Perhaps learning about debt and how it works could open your perspective on how to have a healthy relationship with debt.

2. If I lack money but have drive, is that enough?
Love note: Drive can go a long way! Money can be a result of drive. In my opinion, you can have drive and make money, but if you have neither drive nor money, you will experience stagnation.

State of Mind

1. Do I have a poverty state of mind? That is, do I feel there is only so far and so high I can go?
Love note: Sometimes our environment, meaning how we were raised, can force these negative ideas on us (e.g., you will only be able to succeed so much). If we are told we can't do something because we aren't good enough, we tend to internalize it. If we refuse to accept that we can't do something, and if we act in a positive way to accomplish what we were told we couldn't do, then doesn't that mean we're a true success?

2. Do I think that because my parents were poor, life will be the same for me? If so, how has this mind-set affected me?
Love note: It's scary how much our environment can start to form our self-concept and affect our mind-set. Often we spend half of our lives working at reprogramming our thinking based on our parents' negative perception. On the other hand, the parents who created an environment that built up our self-worth reflect positively on how we view self.

Communication

1. What will I do if a family member wants to borrow a large sum of money? Will I consider myself first?
Love note: It's beautiful to be a giver; however, the greatest gift is giving to yourself and considering the consequences if you don't consider yourself.

2. Do I have a budget?
Love note: You should have a spreadsheet that reflects your weekly or monthly budget. You should also have a savings spreadsheet that itemizes what your

savings are for. For example, "I have $80,000 in savings that we would break down as follows: $20,000 for investments, $10,000 for vacation, $10,000 for car and medical emergencies, $5,000 for continuing education," and so on. Most financial advisers say you need to have the equivalent of one year of wages stashed in a liquid investment account to cover emergencies. They also say you need between 80 and 100 percent of the amount you were making when you were working in order to lead a comfortable life in retirement.

3. Do I have financial baggage? Do I address it in an effort to resolve it?
    Love note: These issues are extremely important to discuss prior to entering a relationship. Hiding your thoughts about these topics hurts both of you.

Financial Options

1. What happens if I suddenly have no income? Do I have a plan for this scenario?
    Love note: If you have savings, part of that money should be set aside for this circumstance. I believe that having a year's salary saved reduces stress drastically.

2. Am I willing to get a second job if needed?
    Love note: There is nothing wrong with additional residual income; it's a win-win as long as they're balanced.

Children and Money

1. What will I teach my kids about money? What are my views?
    Love note: When my daughter was seven, I started teaching her about checking and savings accounts. Now she is in her twenties, has two jobs, takes a full course load at school, and has a retirement account building. My husband and I are now teaching her about investments. Oh, and she is *amazing*! Numerous studies exist that say each kid costs parents between $250,000 and $300,000 before college and weddings. With that said, saving, investing, and budgeting are crucial in this day and age.

2. If I meet someone who I absolutely want to get to know in a vulnerable way and they have kids, will that change my decision to establish a relationship?
    Love note: Children are a blessing, work, and a huge responsibility. Being able to pour into a child's life is a chance for you to extend the best part of yourself so

that a life can be affected. On the other hand, it can be very challenging and a constant reminder that you can't be selfish.

Ayisha's Story

Growing up with eight siblings and raised by a single parent, there usually wasn't enough of anything. With so many people in one house, there never seemed to be enough of the things that mattered. Never enough bath tissue. Never enough soap. Never enough hot water at bath time. At times, there was even not enough food.

My experiences dealing with "not enough" so frequently at such a young age are what taught me to save. I'd always hide a roll or two of bath tissue from each multipack so that we'd always have some on hand. I'd take the remaining soap chips, wet them, and squeeze them together to form a piece large enough to get a few extra showers out of. Looking back, I realize that I wasn't saving anything. What I did was actually a form or hoarding.

Growing up poor and frequently experiencing "not enough" can easily translate into feelings that you are not enough. I couldn't afford to go to a beauty salon to get my hair professionally done, so I didn't feel pretty enough. I didn't wear expensive clothes or shoes, and the first time someone pointed that out, I no longer felt good enough.

I got my first job at fourteen. When I got my first two-week paycheck, I felt rich. Never mind that the check was only for $170; it was more money than I'd ever had. I worked hard for it, and I was proud of my effort. Suddenly, I could buy the things I needed for myself and then some. I finally had enough, and that made me ask if I was enough. With that first paycheck, I promised myself that I'd always be good enough because I'd always have enough. I never wanted to experience "not enough" again, so I became very strict with my spending and savings habits. I told myself that I would always have everything I needed as long as I kept working hard at earning my way through life. I didn't become rich, but I prospered. I worked hard. I earned. I saved. I invested. I had enough, and that was enough.

Reflecting on the "for richer, for poorer" self vow made me realize that I held myself in higher regard during periods of my life when I was earning more money, and I was harder on myself, to the point of not liking myself, when I earned less. Somehow, I'd equated my self-worth with my personal net worth and earning power when I should have loved myself regardless of my circumstances. Loving myself through for richer, for poorer means recognizing that I am enough no matter what my financial situation or emotional state are at certain seasons in life.

Get Ready and Do Your Work!

Whether you are in a poverty state of mind or a challenging financial state, there are options as long as you are willing to make the adjustments. You, the authentic you, are rich and are ready to delete any poverty feelings that you have accepted. Whoever has influenced your poverty state, I suggest that you separate yourself from them, at least until you are healthy. Take time to reset your mind and execute your plan of restructure. You can do this, and remember I'm here with you throughout the process with my tips, exercises, and all the positive energy you can take.

Tips for Shedding a Poverty State of Mind

- Identify your limiting belief.
- Explore avenues to increase your income.
- Educate yourself with financial literature (e.g., books, mentors, courses, and financial events).
- Get more comfortable with words like sales, marketing, and investments.
- Invest wisely.
- Begin an emergency fund.
- Hire a financial coach even if you can only afford it once a month or quarter. You have to start somewhere.

Exercise 1: Putting the Financial Pieces Together

This exercise is to help you get your affairs in order so that when your extension of love shows up, you will be ready and not have to get ready.

1. Record all of your bills and debts on a spreadsheet. Don't hide anything. Remember if anyone, the person you should be able to trust is you.
2. Educate yourself about how money works and how it needs to work for you.
3. Create a budget.
4. Create a savings spreadsheet and allocate amounts for different purposes (e.g., $20,000 savings allocated as follows: medical emergencies, $5,000; vacation, $7,000; car emergencies, $4,000; miscellaneous, $2,000).
5. Make an appointment with a financial coach or financial advisor.
6. Begin to diversify your money.

Reflective Notes

Reflective Notes

Reflective Notes

CHAPTER 5

In Sickness and in Health

Take care of yourself mentally and physically. Even if you go through a short- or long-term illness that causes high levels of pain, don't give up. People who suffer from chronic pain tend to become suicidal. But where there is a will, there is a way; just find the way. Ask yourself if you are compassionate toward others who are sick. If the answer is no, volunteering at a hospital could bring that compassion to the surface. If you find yourself experiencing deep depression, reach out to someone who can help you. Staying committed to your health is vitally important. Go and get your yearly checkup. Eat organic foods in the proper portions. Exercise, get enough sleep, and relieve stress through relaxation. Living this type of life will prepare you for what it takes to keep your vows to another.

In sickness and in health doesn't just mean that you are committing to be there for self if you were to get physically sick; it's also relevant to mental illness as well. Today we are living in a climate in which mental illness is a bigger issue than ever. So many walk around as functional depressed people and sit in silence while suffering behind closed doors. Some are scared of what people would think if they told their truth, and some weren't raised to reach out to a therapist, coach, or spiritual helper.

Whatever the reason, it is important that we commit to being there for self in sickness and in health. If you are diagnosed with a mental or physical illness, that means more than accepting the diagnosis; it also means taking your meds and following up with doctor appointments. That's the commitment to "in health."

Hashani's Story

Hashani is a vibrant and smart young woman who rarely showed her pain and authenticity. Actually, she wouldn't know how to define authenticity, let alone live it. She spent most of her life searching for things to make sense and acceptance. She was so smart and articulate that she hid things that she was deeply hurt by because she was used to being what she thought was perfect.

She had been hurt in one relationship, and she wasn't looking to be in another. That relationship had affected her focus in school, and she was just getting back on her feet and was promoted at her present job. Months later, what was a work friendship resulted in a relationship. She had let her guard down. Something in her knew that she needed to heal what was sick, but she didn't know how, and more than that, she didn't want to. After all, the relationship felt good, and she wanted to ride the love wave. Then came a surprise. She was pregnant, and they committed to being on the journey of family together.

Funny how when there is toxicity in the relationship, specifically the one with self, no news, even good news like a baby coming, can heal inner pain. It can help to heal, but it can't heal it all. We have to do our work. With that said, she went through one of the most hurtful betrayals in a relationship that anyone can go through, specifically when you are carrying his child. She lost it, all the calmness that she worked for years to have. After losing her job and having to move back home, she was now in the phase she resisted and that was feeling. When she began to feel, she began to heal. She was open to being transparent and vulnerable once the pain had consumed every bit of healthy she had left.

She realized that she was ignoring that she had suffered on and off with anxiety. At times she was operating from an unhealthy space mentally by not addressing her anxiety challenges. She knew her relationship with self was sick, and she was desperate to experience healthy. She realized that when she was overwhelmed, her behavior became very assuming, and the what-ifs would lead her down a road of breaking points. Once she began addressing her self-worth, she began to realize that she had to take care of her mind and her soul before she could be a healthy partner, wife, or mother. She knew she needed to separate to elevate to a place of healthy. She moved away for a year and was disconnected from everything familiar. During that time, she grew and she healed.

She fought for her vow of "in sickness and in health." For the next couple of years, I guided her to a much healthier space and to being fearless to unleash her authentic self. The more she healed, the more committed to healthy she became. I'm happy to say, because she stayed committed while things were in a sickness state, she realized that no matter how sick or healthy the situation, she is committed.

The questions in this chapter are essential to fixing a sick relationship with self and how to maintain a healthy outlook with physical sickness.

Self Vows Questions

Commitment

1. What happens if I get sick and decide I want to give up? Are there other options that I have pondered on?
    Love note: Often sick people feel like they will be a burden, but if you are willing to give up, then how can you expect others to fight for your life more than what you are willing to do?

2. Will I stay committed if my potential spouse gets sick and the medical bills pile up? Do I allow bills to pile up in general? If so, how will this behavior affect a potential relationship or the one I'm already in?
    Love note: Please allocate a portion of your savings to health care. Additional insurance will assist with costs that primary insurance doesn't pay for.

3. How will I stay afloat if I've been declared permanently disabled?
    Love note: Unfortunately, disability often barely takes care of your expenses. Having a financial plan if this should occur is key.

4. What if my relationship with self starts to operate as a disease, a cancer, or any other toxin? What are some healthy strategies for handling this?
    Love note: Sometimes we have to take a step back and determine if we are the one who is operating like a cancer. When you are pointing fingers at others, you have three fingers pointing back at you.

5. Am I committed to a healthy lifestyle? If so, how do I define a healthy lifestyle? Is my life operating in a healthy manner?
    Love note: We must define what a healthy lifestyle is, unique to us. Then we must make a commitment and stick to it in sickness and in health.

6. If I have an ailment because I ignored medical advice or chose not to maintain good health, am I keeping my vows to self?
    Love note: You have an obligation to self to take care of yourself the best way you can.

7. Is my relationship with self dysfunctional (i.e., unhealthy)? Am I functioning within the dysfunction (i.e., still unhealthy)?
    Love note: Healthy + unhealthy = unhealthy. Unhealthy + unhealthy = unhealthy. Healthy + Healthy = healthy.

Mental Health

1. Is my body healthy? Do I get a yearly physical? Do I put healthy foods into my body? Do I have a workout regimen? Do I feed my mind with balanced and enriching thoughts?
    Love note: Answering yes to all of these questions is an indicator that you are committed to the vow of "in sickness and in health."

2. Are my emotions healthy? Healthy is the ability to be balanced and navigate in a healthy manner through conflict. It is also to be okay with not being okay. It's having compassion and being kind to yourself despite what others may do to you. Explain.
    Love note: Any form of codependence in a relationship is unhealthy.

3. How will I respond if I am diagnosed with a mental illness such as bipolar disorder or schizophrenia? Will I keep my commitment of good health, refuse to seek out healthy alternatives, or refuse to take prescribed medicine?
    Love note: You are beautiful whether you have a mental or physical illness or not, and your power within will see you through.

4. Do I have any type of illness that could affect my relationship with self or my relationships with others?
    Love note: This information is vitally important. If you don't acknowledge it, refuse to follow doctors' orders, or refuse to be truthful about this information to yourself or your partner, you are taking away your partner's ability to make informed decisions about your relationship.

5. Am I dedicated to my well-being and how my answer affects others?
    Love note: If your words, actions, and intentions come from a place opposite of well-being, you are not committed to your well-being or how it affects others.

6. Are my decisions usually sound, or am I easily distracted by the noise of life? If I am easily distracted, what or who tends to distract me? How can I address these distractions?

Love note: Distractions can be a much needed interruption or cause us to stay unfocused. Interruptions that cause us to pause and redirect so that we can get on the right path are some of the best gifts.

Family History

1. Does anyone in my family suffer from alcoholism or drug addiction? If so, how has that affected my views on alcohol and drugs?
   Love note: Alcoholism or drug addiction is a sickness that can affect how we show up in the world even if we are not the ones who are addicted. Being a survivor of a loved one who has been through it causes us to be affected by the journey.

2. If one or both of my parents get ill, would I consider taking them in to live with me?
   Love note: We never want to face this or think about it because our parents are like superheroes, but one day we will, and it's best that we have a plan.

3. What is my medical history, including that of my family?
   Love note: Knowing the medical history of your partner is important, especially regarding hereditary conditions.

Self-Health

1. If my doctor recommended that I change my diet because of medical concerns, would I be willing to do it?
   Love note: Change is good when it's for the better. Sometimes we need to pack up the negative and move it out; other times it may be just a fine-tuning, such as decreasing sugar and increasing vegetables.

2. Am I dedicated to being my healthiest self, physically and mentally? How will I do that?
   Love note: I did not know where to start when I wanted to get healthy, and I was overwhelmed. However, finding a health coach helped me, along with reading.

3. Am I dedicated to self-help? Do I take any self-help courses or attend any wellness retreats?
   Love note: If you want to be pampered for three days and two nights, and divorce the fake self and marry the authentic self, please check out michellerhannah.com

under retreats and sign up for a one-on-one interview with our retreat team. We would love for you to join us!

4. How do I feel about therapy or coaching?
   Love note: Regardless of your preconceived notions about either, if you have the right therapist or coach for you, it can be absolutely life changing.

Amber's Story

It was 1999, I was nineteen years old, and I was finally getting my life back on track after leaving my mother's house at seventeen. After feeling as though life had chewed me up and spit me out, I had a nice job, a car, and I had re-enrolled at Santa Monica College. I was in a good place.

College offered free services, one being birth control, so I decided to take advantage of it. I wanted to be totally independent and off my mother's insurance.

I went to the clinic and received a pelvic exam. While in the midst of the exam, the doctor felt something in my stomach. To my surprise, she seemed pretty adamant that I was pregnant. I assured her that I was not pregnant because I regularly took birth control. She requested that I follow up the next day at her private facility for another examination. I went to the exam, and she said, "You have something in there, and you need to go to your primary physician and get examined."

I made a visit to my doctor's office, and they confirmed that I had a tumor attached to my ovary that needed to be removed quickly, namely the following weekend. I told my mother that I was going to have surgery, and she adamantly objected. I didn't return to the doctor and continued to postpone appointments. I just thought it would go away if I didn't face it.

Finally, after I had missed about three appointments, the doctor's office called and questioned the reasoning behind missing the appointments. I replied that my schedule was hectic and I'd be at the next one. After getting off the phone with the nurse, I felt conflicted because in that moment I knew that I wasn't committed to the self vow "in sickness and in health." I asked myself what I was going to do about it. I decided I would definitely make the next appointment. The phone rang again, and it was the nurse saying the doctor wanted me to come now and that he would wait for me. I immediately got up and went to the appointment. Once I arrived, I began to cry because I knew that I had been avoiding the truth as it related to my body. I was also burdened by the series of events that had taken place since I moved out of my mother's house

By the time my surgery was scheduled, I had a five-pound tumor attached to my ovary. When signing the consent form for surgery, I read that it could result in an ovariectomy of one or possibly two ovaries. I objected immediately, specifically because I wanted children and if I needed to harvest my eggs, I would do so. The doctor at that moment was horrible and told me that I could die. He asked me, "What do you want us to do? Remove the one, close you back up, wake you up, and ask you if we can take the other one?" I said, "Yes, that is exactly what I want you to do." I already knew of a young woman who had a hysterectomy, and I didn't want that narrative over my life.

The consent form was amended. I signed it and proceeded to surgery. After the surgery, my mother later told me that it was *cancer*. Ignorance is bliss. I was not afraid. I thought, *Okay, so I'll lose my hair. I can grow it back. I'm not going to die.*

I never thought that I was going to die. However, the experience felt as though my body and emotions were imprisoned. I just wanted to isolate myself, take my treatment, and do my time just like a prison. I had four rounds of chemotherapy on my first visit to chemo. I was expected to be there for eight hours. I took with me a word search, a CD player, a bag of chips, a salad, and an orange juice. Again, ignorance is bliss. I walked out with a paper bag for the nausea.

I would have to endure chemo five days in a row for four months. The first day was eight hours, and the following days were two to four hours. I was ridiculously sick the first week, with nausea, fatigue, and aching bones. The next week, I was half as sick, a third as sick the following week, and back to normal the fourth week, just in time to start it all over again.

My mother would drive me on Mondays, and I would cry the whole way to the doctor's office because I knew what was coming. Thank God I had support, and who better than your mom!

I remember at nineteen reflecting on all of the things that I thought were important and how insignificant they were to me now. One particular memory was of the yearbooks I had my classmates sign, and my thought was that if I were to die, it wouldn't be important to anyone. I felt I was irrelevant.

Eventually, I finished the chemo, my hair grew back, and I went on with my life. However, this time, as I was reintroduced into the world, it would never be the same. I had changed and evolved deeply. Life would forever have the footprint of cancer and chemo.

That two-year chemo journey, which felt like a prison sentence, was my worst. Everything was better than those days. I became an optimist because I knew that there were people who went through what I went through but didn't survive. I survived, so I am immensely blessed. I am blessed, I have a reason to smile, I have a reason to live, and

I have a reason to say that today is a better day. I didn't say today was a great day or the best day, but I know one thing for sure, and that is that today is not the worst, and for that I am grateful. I am also grateful for my smile and that I can keep going.

It was not an option to stay committed in my worst of times. I knew that I had to stand in the midst of the pain because somehow I knew that I deserved to live. I knew that my better would be defined for the rest of my life. If I didn't know what my worst was, I wouldn't realize what better truly meant to me. The active fight to survive cancer was physically, mentally, and emotionally overwhelming. When I think back to my worst chemotherapy days, I think about the constant vomiting, the fatigue, the lack of sleep, and the void it created in my life.

Now on the other side of the disease, I have made a conscious decision to be a light. The fact that I survived gave me an idea of the concept of true sickness. It stood as a weight on my scale. Everything became comparable to my worst day on chemo, and I have yet to have a day as bad as those days. Therefore, I have a reason to smile and be positive. What if I had given up in sickness? I would never have known what it was to feel healthy. The truth is, I wouldn't be here as a survivor, which means I'm still here to tell the tale! My world is for healthy, positive, and prosperous because I'm still here. I get the opportunity every morning to have an amazing story to live and tell. I made it through sickness, and I live daily in health!

Get Ready to Get to Work

"In sickness and in health" is such a personal vow to me. I have lived it. Standing here as a cancer survivor, a survivor of the last six years of chronic pain, and someone with canal dehiscence and slight memory loss, I have committed to this vow over and over again. It's been rough, and at times I have felt like giving up on me, but I have realized that Michelle R. Hannah is so loved. I love her with the illnesses and all of their effects. I love her when she is operating in total health and during the days when the unhealthy creeps in. I encourage you to commit to "in sickness and in health." It may be tough, but again, I have some tips and exercises, and I'm emphasizing the importance of identifying and eliminating stress triggers. Stress is at the foundation of most illnesses, so it's important to eliminate our stress. Besides, stress doesn't connect to anything healthy.

Tips: Identify and Eliminate Stress Triggers

Stress harms both your mind and your body. At some point in life, we all will be affected by stress, whether internally or externally imposed. Stress can lead to bad decision-making, depression, consistent arguing, physical ailments, and more. Consider these tips to prevent or address stress:

- Identify the triggers of your stress. For example, being yelled at can trigger one to shut down and therefore hold in important things by not communicating. Keeping things inside causes stress.
- Reflect on preventing these triggers. If you can't prevent the triggers, then discuss options to prevent the stress.
- Reflect on how you will support yourself with stress triggers. For example, if you have someone in your circle who consistently triggers you, then perhaps figuring out your boundaries and expectations to offset the effect of stress would be effective.

Consider this scenario: Shannon gets very stressed when she feels she is running late and begins to snap at the people around her. Leaving earlier or looking at traffic patterns before leaving could decrease her stress. In addition, listening to relaxing music could counter stress when an unexpected accident or traffic occurs.

Every stress trigger has a solution, even if it is not obvious at first. Think about your options and choose the best solutions for your situation.

Exercise: Morning Meditation

1. Steal away to a place that is quiet and feels safe. This will usher in the calm.
2. Disconnect from distractions (e.g., technology, TV, phone). This will eliminate the anxiety associated with stress.
3. Be committed to the process of meditation. Listen to your inner voice or compass.
4. Set a time that you are committing (e.g., fifteen minutes, thirty minutes, an hour, etc.).
5. Don't get up until you feel that the burdens or concerns are no longer heavy and controlling how you show up in the world. Releasing all negativity is great for your overall physical health.

Reflective Notes

Reflective Notes

Reflective Notes

CHAPTER 6

To Love and to Cherish

We often hear the advice, "Love yourself first," but you can't do that if you don't like yourself or if you haven't defined love. If you don't value yourself or think that you are worthy, how do you expect to cherish someone else or to be cherished? It took me years to like myself. I had to go through my own journey. First, I had to become aware that something was wrong. I had to tell myself the truth no matter how bad, shameful, or hurtful it was. Once I liked myself, I started to fall in love with me, and eventually I loved myself. Naturally, life still happened, and I had my days of feeling that no one loved me, but I picked myself up. You have to be able to do that for yourself before you can share love with someone else and cherish your partner from a healthy space.

Love is all there is! This year, at the end of a session with a few of my clients, I found myself suffering from a ministroke and heart attack symptoms. I felt as if my life were slipping away. I remember being in the ambulance and thinking, *Wow. I may never see my daughter, husband, or mother again.* I asked myself if I had loved enough. Had I loved myself enough? Had I let unforgiveness keep me from loving enough? I couldn't talk accept a little slurring, but oh could I feel. I realized in that moment that love was all there is. It was all that mattered. I committed that if I could just live through it, I would love deeper, like today is tomorrow, and with total grace before it was even asked. I would forgive daily and grant myself a do-over each day. Love is patient. Love is patient. Love is patient. Did I mention that love is patient? So be patient with yourself, and it will be easier to be patient with others.

Mike's Story

Coming from the dangerous gang surroundings of the inner city of Compton affected how Mike viewed himself and how others viewed him. Although he grew up in a home in which his parents loved him, promoted education, and had morals and structure, he still succumbed to gangbanging and lack of self-worth. He was literally living two lives: a preppy kid on one hand and a gang member participant on the other.

Anytime he was outside of his area, he felt that he was less than because of how he looked and his race. He determined this by the way others treated him, the stares of hierarchy, and the consistent stops by the police department. Keep in mind that when Mike was outside his area, he was well-dressed, respectful, and followed his parents' rules. However, after so many of these hurtful situations, he began to live how he was treated and started to get involved in gang activity. Despite his positive home life, he still succumbed to things that were results from the inner city. The manner in which the neighborhood, the media, and other races portrayed young black males infused the anger he felt, and his lack of self-worth fueled a lack of care for human life and feelings.

In an attempt to channel his energy in a different direction, he went into the military in hopes that it would change his lack of self-worth and value. The result was that he just became a gangbanger within the military. You see, if we don't change from within, moving to an entirely different country won't make a difference because we take self with us. I believe there are breaking points that happen in life that feel like a jolt. Whether we surrender to the paradigm shifts is up to us.

A man in the military approached Mike and asked, "Why do you act this way?" It was the first time someone had asked him that at that phase of his life. Within that same time period, one morning he woke on a bench after being intoxicated and realized that he was numbing his pain and acting out his anger in an unhealthy way. Those two wake-up calls started his transition away from a lack of self-love.

Mike started to learn about where he came from culturally, and in spite of the psychological effects of slavery that were passed down from generation to generation, he began to have a different perspective on what his ancestors had accomplished and endured. He began to dig deeper and uncover all the reasons why his self-worth was low and, in some areas, nowhere to be found. He realized that there was a connection between history and him feeling relevant and confident. He came from a long line of inventors, doctors, lawyers, healers, activists, and historians, and that was enough to discredit the narrative that was imposed on him.

The next breaking point for Mike was losing his beloved mother after a decade of taking care of her. Life has a way of preparing you for the next step if you allow it. He was now ready to move to emotional intimacy with self and begin to fall in love with self. The night his mom transitioned, I witnessed someone I had known for thirty years surrender to vulnerability. God knows what we need in order to elevate. Sometimes the deepest loss can force us to take a long look at self and begin to navigate through our choice to be transparent. He made the choice to become intimate with self. He embraced every truth and disconnected from every fear of disappointment, pain, and grief.

He realized he didn't trust himself and that was at the core of why he didn't trust others and proceeded with extreme caution in most conversations, specifically with anything that would expose the real him. By increasing his self-worth and surrendering to emotional intimacy, he realized that it was too draining to keep the stone wall of emotions up.

The more he liked and loved himself, the more he began to see the reflection of his truth in the love that surrounded him in his support circle. In the past, because of his robotic behavior, he had attracted people who were robotic, making him feel that his behavior was okay and that was the way life was supposed to be. However, once he allowed love for self to settle within his heart, he allowed his healthy relationships to penetrate, correct, and expand emotional intimacy.

He finally took the vows to self that he would love and cherish through consistent trust, openness to vulnerability, honesty, and fearlessness. Although I would love to end it here, transparency also means exposing the challenges that occur after one takes the self vows, specifically to love and to cherish. To love and to cherish, operating at its healthiest is unconditional. I like to say that if you want to experience unconditional self-love, stop putting conditions on it. The healthy side is that Mike is more connected to self-intimacy, which allows him to connect on a deeper level of honesty.

Mike has always struggled with self-sabotage regarding his finances. It affects him deeply in his relationship with self-love and self-care. After a major loss once again, he has realized that ego and the lack of total surrender and full transparency with self has prevented him from immersing self in self-love and cherishing his blessing. The hope is that he is now ready to overcome the challenges and do his self-work. The beauty is that he gets a do-over every day. For this I'm thankful.

Self Vows Questions

Let It Go

1. Do I keep score of everything that has happened to me? If so, how does this impact my relationship with self?

Love note: Keeping score is holding on to the pain or disappointment associated with the incident. You deserve to be free and have a do-over every time you want to do something better. You can make the choice to give yourself a second chance.

2. Do I allow pride to prevent me from apologizing? If so, is the outcome favorable?
Love note: I apologize to self all the time. I offend myself daily. It could be that I'm apologizing for a lack of compassion or doing something that is not representing my true self. An apology is a statement to turn away from what I just did that was offensive or hurtful.

3. Am I easily angered? Do I make people feel that they have to walk on eggshells around me?
Love note: If people have to walk on eggshells and can't confide in you for fear of a negative reaction, they can't be themselves and trust is compromised.

Support

1. Am I sarcastic in an attempt to cover up my true feelings?
Love note: Reflect on how you feel when you are mocked, and ask yourself if it's okay that you inflict that negative experience on self.

2. Am I self-centered, or do I always think about the well-being of the relationship?
Love note: Love is unselfish, and it will wait until you get it right! Care about *getting* it right, not about *being* right.

3. What are some things that could improve my relationship with self?
Love note: Make a list of what you would like to improve, even if it's just a little bit more.

4. Do I get jealous of the accomplishments of others?
Love note: Love is not jealous; it does not envy.

Conflict Resolution

1. If I were to fall out of love with myself, what steps would I take to address the problem?
Love note: It's not a bad thing to fall out of love with self when self is toxic.

2. What is my biggest fear about being in a relationship?
    Love note: When we can't have a relationship with self, it's impossible to have a relationship with others.

3. What is the best way to keep love alive in a relationship with self or others?
    Love note: If you are waking up feeling dead, then there's no way possible you can feel alive in a relationship. Sure, there may be some moments of joy, but overall it is up to us to decide to live and not just survive. Every day can be a new birth of self. The choice is yours.

Special Occasions

1. How important to me are special occasions such as birthdays and wedding anniversaries? Do I celebrate myself, or do I wait for others?
    Love note: Birthdays are such a gift. It's an entire twelve months that you have lived through, and guess what? You have a chance at another year! But in the meantime, let's just celebrate the day!

2. How do I usually spend my downtime? Do I have fun? What is an ideal weekend?
    Love note: Commit today to fifteen minutes of fun. It's important to have fun every day in our lives, and you don't have to wait for official downtime to have it.

Commitment

1. Do I believe the love I have for myself can pull me through anything? If not, what are some challenges that love might not conquer?
    Love note: Relationships can be challenging, but the overcoming is so worth it.

2. Do I give up when I'm facing several challenges?
    Love note: If you give up when things don't go your way, then I would bet that your relationships are not reaching their full potential either.

Vanessa's Story

I grew up in a household in which my mom was very into her children; she was emotionally intimate. However, a very special man in my life was emotionally abusive. I knew he loved me, but the way he showed it truly damaged me. I realize now that it paved the way for how I relate to men in relationships. I realize now that I didn't truly know what love was. How could I love anyone when I didn't love myself? My self-esteem is so low, and I realize it started with that special man calling me dumb and stupid and questioning my self-worth.

So many nights I have thought that I just want to be loved, but on the other hand, I'm scared. After several years of being in a relationship, the person I truly loved didn't love me enough to marry me. As it turned out, he was cheating on me, and that hurt me deeply. There is still a part of me that's hurt.

I am shut down and disconnected, and I didn't realize how much until the Self Vows Retreat. Once I was in the seminars, heard the other stories, and thought about my own feelings, I knew I questioned my value. The more I sat there, the more I knew how scared I was to be transparent and vulnerable.

As I listened to the definitions of the vows and attempted to complete the exercises, I realized how much of a stranger I was to myself. I want to be married, but how can I vow to love and cherish someone when I don't show that to self? Cherish means to treat someone like he or she is a prized possession, but if I don't treat myself like a treasure, then providing that or expecting that from someone else is not realistic.

The day of our self vows ceremony, it hit me so hard and penetrated my soul deeply that I was ready to love and cherish myself first. I needed some time to do that before moving on to another. I have since committed to the process of self-love, and not only does it feel like home, but it has also increased my business presence.

Get Ready to Do Your Work

Tips for Quality Time

When you learn to like yourself, you will be intrigued to find out more and more about yourself. As you spend more time with you, falling in love is imminent. Once you love yourself inside and out, you will run toward spending quality time with self instead of running away. There's something about unleashing your authenticity that goes hand in hand with the vow to love and cherish. These simple tips will help make you further define the beauty of self.

- Every night before you go to sleep, spend some time with self without the TV on. Unplug from technology and plug in to self.
- Focus on what you're feeling and need. Sometimes the distraction is just too loud. It's okay to quiet it down for a much-needed moment.
- It's these quiet moments that deeply connect you more and more to authenticity and love for self.

Exercise for Acceptance

If you are ready to truly pull off the layers and do the challenging work of acceptance and truth, then this exercise will start you on that journey. I know this one may be a little scary and intimidating, but I promise if you stick it out, the gift you will receive will be so worth it.

1. Get undressed. Remove everything so that you are in your birthday suit.
2. Stand in front of the mirror.
3. For five minutes, I want you to say every thought that comes to your mind. (*Love note:* If you can't do five, start with two minutes. Just get started.)
4. After you have completed your two to five minutes, state three affirmations or positive statements about yourself.
5. Repeat, "I love you," until the anxiety or any ill feelings start to dissipate.

Reflective Notes

Reflective Notes

Reflective Notes

CHAPTER 7

To Love and to Cherish through Intimacy

Intimacy is the experience of connection to another person. In this chapter, I will be focusing on self-intimacy. Self-intimacy means accepting all facets of self, including the areas that make you uncomfortable, insecure, shameful, or vulnerable. When you are not afraid to let go, you are no longer inhibited.

According to Coleen L., "Emotional intimacy is a psychological state that occurs when the trust and communication level between people fosters the mutual sharing of each other's innermost self. It is unbridled mutual self-disclosure."[7] However, I want to focus on embracing and developing emotional intimacy with self. Emotional intimacy with yourself is being willing to be with your feelings fully as they arise without trying to distract yourself or push them down. If you are ready to take the intimacy journey and begin trusting yourself, please know that it's very important to trust self first. When you trust self, you will spend less time vacillating.

Jay's Story

Jay had no clue what intimacy was and was totally clueless on what that meant in a relationship. He had to *trust* the process, and that process would require him to embrace another word, which was vulnerability.

Jay was in a new relationship, and he knew within weeks that she was the one. He connected with her on the deepest level that surpassed what he thought was possible.

---

[7] Coleen L., "Emotional Intimacy," https://www.selfgrowth.com/articles/ColeenL1.html.

The only issue was he didn't know how to show it or communicate it. He knew how to communicate financials, concepts, formulas, and anything on the surface. He took some major steps out of his comfort zone, but it wasn't going to last for a long-term relationship. He needed to grow and evolve and not just stay neutral and safe. After all, the woman he felt he had fallen in love with was open, vulnerable, transparent, risk-taking, and a little feisty at times. She was open to shaking things up, and he was most comfortable with balance and playing it safe. As it turned out, she needed more of what he had and he needed a whole lot of what she had as it related to self-intimacy, vulnerability, transparency, communication, and being comfortable with honesty.

He started to realize that he wasn't self-intimate; he actually ran away from his innermost feelings. As he looked more deeply into self, he came to understand that he was never taught how to communicate effectively about his feelings or that it was okay to show the vulnerability needed for self-love. He thought about how he grew up in a neighborhood where there was little trust, no men cried, and talking about your feelings was considered soft. He had been programmed to think this way for thirty-eight years until love showed up.

As his mate began to teach him more about self-intimacy, the benefits, and the steps on how to get there, he was on a seesaw of emotions. Two of those emotions in particular were resistance and surrender. Some days he resisted, and those were his most difficult with self and his relationship. The days he surrendered, he was more compassionate, kind, and loving to self. Coincidently, it was the same in his relationship. He realized that how he showed up for self was strongly connected to how he showed up in the relationship.

After many debates, thoughts of breaking up, and disagreements, he came to understand that the more he was closed in some areas, the further he moved away from intimacy. Once he submitted to transparency and honesty, it was easier to be vulnerable. He started to be clear about who he was. Some things he hated and was ashamed of, and some he felt empowered by, like he was more than a conqueror.

He was finally able to show up fully, trusting self and his choices. He was open to giving everything about who he was because he gave it to himself first. You can't give what you don't have … He embraced the journey of liking and loving himself, in turn he was all in for taking the journey to like and love his mate. He knew that his capacity for love had come from a superficial place. After all, many relationships are on the surface until the veil is pulled off. We then realize that we haven't truly loved with the intention of loving unconditionally.

This was a special story to tell for this reason: Jay is my husband, and I am so happy to have been the one to guide him through this journey. It elevated my commitment to love and to cherish—the ultimate selfless act.

There are eight intimacies that are commonly spoken about, but I will be focusing on four that I utilize the most with couples and singles. Those intimacies are emotional, intellectual, physical, and spiritual intimacy.

Emotional Intimacy

We desire to be accepted and share our love with one another. We want to know that in tough times, we can be vulnerable and transparent with another. That's emotional intimacy. We crave closeness, trust, and safety. We need and want a special connection with another on a deep emotional level.

Many couples can be married for years and not achieve emotional intimacy. It truly takes effort and commitment to achieve. Don't think of it as a destination but a journey of evolution and experiencing a deeper connection.

Self Vows Questions

Vulnerability

1. When I think of the word *vulnerable*, how do I feel?
   Love note: The word *vulnerable* makes me smile now, but it used to make me cringe because I wasn't used to standing in my truth. But now I love standing in the light.

2. When was the last time I cried with no judgment of myself? Do I think it's weak to cry? If so, where did this thought come from?
   Love note: Have you ever been told not cry and to be strong as if it were weak to shed some tears? Crying is healing. It's such a release, and I want you to release.

3. Do I hide my flaws? If so, what are my flaws, and why do I hide them?
   Love note: Remember your flaws are your beauty, and the absence of it is a flaw in itself.

4. If I could narrate my story in this moment, what would it say?
   Love note: Stand in front of the mirror and narrate your story for twenty minutes. Is it accurate? Concentrate on the most treasured, intimate, embarrassing memories and the stories that you are most scared to share.

5. If I could change anything about the way I was raised, what would it be?
   Love note: I believe we would all change things, but I also believe that even the mistakes have built character and taught us great lessons.

Communication and Trust

1. Am I afraid to talk to myself about anything? If so, what are those things?
    Love note: When you expose your fears, you are better able to overcome them. However, if you are afraid to share openly with yourself, you will be scared to share them with someone else.

2. Is there any way in which I *don't* trust my decisions? Do I have any doubts about the future? If so, what are they?
    Love note: It's normal to have some doubt. You should be able to discuss anything without fear of judgment. It's such a relief when you tell someone something that you were very afraid to say and the person's response is a hug instead of judgment.

3. I am scared for a potential partner to find out … (fill in the blank)
    Love note: It's tough being vulnerable, but it's necessary to be transparent. Choose wisely with vulnerability, but always stand in your truth. Your truth is beautiful, and love recognizes love.

4. Before making a telephone call, do I ever rehearse what I am going to say? Why or why not?
    Love note: Some phone calls related to business may need a little rehearsing if you are reading from a script, but when it's personal, no rehearsal is needed, just authenticity.

5. What are my greatest accomplishments in life? What makes them the greatest?
    Love note: Take a step back and write down all of your accomplishments. Write a *G* by the ones you feel are truly great. I'll give you one to start you off: you made it this far in this book, and that is great.

Intellectual Intimacy

Intellectual intimacy can be toward self or another person. You must be aware of your goals, dreams, and visions as an individual before you can ever share intellectual intimacy with another. Intellectual intimacy is comfortably being aware of ideas, goals, and visions. It is also beautiful when you can share dreams, visions, and goals with one another and communicate about similarities and differences. If you can do this in a comfortable manner, then you can experience a deep level of intellectual intimacy. It is important not to judge one another for your ideas, thoughts, goals, and visions because when judgment is present, openness cannot shine. You might not agree with all of your partner's beliefs and thoughts, but sharing the gift of freedom is priceless. Differences are good because they allow us to see things from a totally new perspective. Intellectual intimacy happens when there is no fear of being demeaned or dismissed.

Action Plans, Goals, and SWOT Analysis

Action plans, goals, and SWOT analysis are very important tools to help us figure out how to connect to intellectual intimacy both as an individual and as a couple.

Action Plans

Action plans help people know what needs to be done to complete a task, project, initiative, or strategy. An action plan generally includes steps, milestones, and measures of progress, as well as responsibilities, specific assignments, and a timeline.

To create an action plan, follow these steps:

- Define the problem(s).
- Collect and analyze the data.
- Identify the individual tasks and order them by priority.
- Identify any challenges, barriers, and self-defeating tendencies.
- Focus on priorities and what is due now.
- Clarify and prioritize the problem(s).
- Write a goal statement for each solution.
- Implement solutions (a.k.a. the action plan).
- Monitor and evaluate.
- Identify the individual tasks and order them by priority.
- Determine who can help you.

Goal-Setting

Goals are defined as observable and measurable end results that have one or more objectives to be achieved within a more or less fixed timeframe.

Use this process to set achievable goals:

- Use a goal-setting worksheet and goal planner.
- Think through and identify your goals.

- Determine whether each goal is a short-term goal (e.g., six months) or a long-term goal (e.g., one year or more)
- Prioritize goals.
- Choose with one goal to start with.
- Create an action plan to achieve your goal.
- Break down your goal action plan into manageable baby steps.
- Set a due date.
- Don't procrastinate.
- Visualize your intentions as accomplished.
- Find quotes, people, or situations that inspire you and keep you motivated.
- Ensure that your surroundings support your goals.
- Be aware that you will have obstacles, so a plan to overcome them as needed.
- Get excited! Success is a process, but this goal is a step toward bigger goals that equate to bigger dreams and visions.

SWOT Analysis

Creating a personal SWOT analysis focused on self-awareness is the key to creating the success you want in your personal and business goals. For the purposes of this book, we will focus on the personal goals. SWOT stands for strengths, weakness, opportunities, and threats.

Couples who have used SWOT analysis for their goals as a couple have experienced measurable and beneficial results. I had completed several SWOT analyses for my business before I completed my first one for my personal life. I am so glad I did; it has proven equally beneficial for both my husband and me.

Self-awareness is key to how we make decisions that are crucial to our businesses and lives. First you must identify the opportunities, but once you do, don't wait for the door to open. Open it yourself. In some cases, kick it down.

Let's get started with your personal SWOT analysis.

1. Strengths. Strengths are things that truly light you up and energize you.
   - What are your strengths?
   - How can you utilize your strengths more?
   - How do your strengths create opportunity to reach your full potential?

2. Weaknesses (a.k.a. opportunities to grow). Weaknesses are the things that zap your energy, even if you are good at doing them.

- How can you reduce or eliminate your weaknesses by leveraging them as opportunities for growth?
- What steps will you take to eliminate your weaknesses and turn them into opportunities to grow?
- What other weaknesses could these opportunities introduce?

3. Opportunities. Opportunities are the things that will drive your personal and professional impact and growth.
    - What are your opportunities?
    - Which key opportunities will accelerate your impact and growth?
    - What resources and support do you need to create these opportunities?

4. Threats. Threats are anything that can cause damage to your personal or professional life. This is anything that could intrude on your peace and success in your personal and professional life. Although threats are negative, they can be redirected into a positive.
    - What are the threats that present obstacles to accomplishing your goals?
    - What are your limiting beliefs and negative self-talk around your goals?
    - How can you transition to empowering beliefs and positive self-talk?
    - What positive affirmations can you use to help counter these threats?

When I went through this process, self-reflection and answering these SWOT questions helped me to both open my self-awareness and become more aware of the world around me. By uncovering the opportunities and threats in your personal life, you can prevent many situations that can be damaging to your growth. Still not convinced? Here are a few benefits of creating your own personal SWOT:

- Helps you develop strategies to attain your goals.
- Shows where you currently stand on the path to success.
- Measures the scope of reaching your desired goals.
- Enhances your career, life, and personality.
- Ushers you into a deeper authenticity of who you are personally and professionally.
- Maximizes your strengths and provides an opportunity to grow from your weaknesses.
- Helps you understand your preferences and personality traits.
- Focuses on your attitudes, abilities, skills, capabilities, and capacities.

Self Vows Questions

Purpose

1. What is my purpose? How do I know that this is my purpose?
   Love note: Purpose, in my opinion, is not found but unleashed, so unleash it today!

2. What is my vision for a strong relationship with self?
   Love note: Having a vision goes hand in hand with having goals. So write your vision down.

Communication

1. Do I consistently have intellectually stimulating conversations in my head or out loud with myself?
   Love note: Whether it's in your head or aloud, it's very important to voice your thoughts and stimulate your mind daily.

2. Do I challenge myself to bring up a variety of topics? Explain the process that takes place when you challenge yourself.
   Love note: Don't skip steps. You'll only have to take the test over.

3. Do I have weekly brainstorming sessions in an effort to achieve my life goals?
   Love note: Brainstorming is great for getting your thoughts out and visualizing how those ideas will increase or decrease your happiness, balance, and overall peace.

Spiritual Intimacy

Don Harvey, author of *The Spiritually Intimate Marriage*, defines spiritual intimacy as being able to share your spiritual self, find it reciprocated, and have a sense of union with your mate.[8] Just because you go to church, read the scripture, or pray doesn't mean that you have spiritual intimacy. Individually you must seek to know God's will, to be close to God, and to submit to His will. Spiritual intimacy is immensely powerful, and it energizes us when life seems hopeless.

When we are open, we don't feel the need or the pressure to cover up! It's scary to be spiritually naked, but think about how you feel when you have told the truth or exposed

---

[8] Don Harvey, *The Spiritually Intimate Marriage* (Kentwood, MI: Baker Books, 1991).

a secret you have been hiding. The bottom line is that you feel free! To be open is to walk hand in hand with freedom!

Self Vows Questions

Relationship

1. How has the power of God broken destructive patterns in my life?
   Love note: Spiritual connection has a way of breaking things up that don't need to be in our lives and allowing us to see things more clearly.

2. Am I open to letting God use my strengths and weaknesses?
   Love note: If you are not open to God using your strengths and weaknesses, then how do you utilize them?

Spiritual Connection

1. Do I ever sit and just listen to God's voice?
   Love note: Sitting quietly is the best because you can hear your spirit, align with your truth, and allow God to speak.

2. How do I connect spiritually to self (whatever this personally means to you)?
   Love note: I connect in so many ways spiritually to self, perhaps because I am in total surrender to God. I feel it through gratitude, kindness, love, quiet, forgiveness, etc.

3. What is God calling me to do with my life?
   Love note: This question is very complex and each answer is unique to each individual.

4. What three spiritual qualities connect me with living my best spiritual self?
   Love note: If you don't know three spiritual qualities, write the ones you want to have.

Physical Intimacy

Physical intimacy is a sexual, sensual, physical connection in which you share reactions, thoughts, emotions, and inhibitions. This connection can include behaviors such as kissing, holding hands, hugging, caressing, and sexual activity. Physical intimacy is not just being physical. Remember it's a form of intimacy.

Being physically intimate with self can mean massaging your own body, being naked, hugging yourself every morning, and giving yourself amazing head rubs. Once you master this type of intimacy for self, it will be organic to share it with another. Communication is vital; you have to talk to one another about what pleases you and what doesn't. It's so much deeper than just the act of having sex. When you love someone, being physical with him or her is an exciting and adventurous exploration of the bodily journey. It's especially wonderful when you are experiencing this with your life partner because you can take your time. There's no rush; you have the rest of your lives!

Self Vows Questions

Communication

1. How do I communicate when I'm not satisfied sexually?
   Love note: Knowing your body comes first and foremost. Sharing what your needs and wants are is just as important.

2. What are my views on infidelity?
   Love note: If you cheat yourself, then you can't expect someone else to not cheat. Remember we attract who we are.

3. How often do I want to be physically intimate?
   Love note: Physical intimacy is important, and figuring out your vision for physical intimacy is a part of your empowerment.

Affection

1. What roles do love and affection play in my life?
   Love note: Affection expressed physically makes friendship complete and binding. Start focusing more on establishing a friendship.

2. If I am in a relationship, is it physical enough for both of us? What would make it better?
   Love note: Communication is key and knowing yourself is essential.

3. How and where do I like to be touched?
   Love note: Remember it's not about what *you* prefer; it's about how your partner feels too. Hint: Your partner knows his or her body and what he or she likes best. Just ask.

4. What are some things my partner and I can do outside the bedroom to keep the feelings of intimacy going all day?

   Love note: Remember physical intimacy is only one part of intimacy, but the intimacy outside of the bedroom is truly where the fireworks happen.

5. What would I do if I were diagnosed with a sexual disorder?

   Love note: Seeking help and exploring the options with your mate is a gesture of love, commitment, and emotional intimacy. Don't be afraid to explore the options and be transparent with your fears and concerns. Love is so much deeper than sex.

Giving the Gift of Intimacy

What are the guidelines or requirements for intimacy? One is confidence. Another is the ability to trust yourself and others. In order for anyone to truly know you, you have to believe you are worth knowing. You have to respect yourself, honor yourself, be honest with yourself, and have your own back before you can ask someone else to do the same. You have to give yourself the gift of dating yourself first. As a result, you will be able to give what you long to receive. When this process occurs, it is perhaps the greatest gift we as human beings can give ourselves and our partners: the gift of ourselves intimately.

Have you ever heard the phrase "the gift of giving"? When you give of yourself openly and freely, you give the greatest gift because you give the authentic you! Keep in mind that you have to listen to your soul, and you can't give yourself intimately to just anybody. Your soul will lead you to the right place.

The Five Love Languages by Dr. Gary Chapman is one of the most effective tools I use with couples. It is an eye-opener for both parties. As I began to look more closely at the love languages, I realized that we must demonstrate our individual love languages to self before we expect someone to love us how we need to be loved and vice versa.

I like my clients to choose their top two love languages and find a way to speak them to self. For example, if one of your love languages is acts of service, then cook your favorite meal for yourself. If your other love language is gifts, then buy a gift for you. You can even have a sales associate wrap it. This may sound a little silly, but that's only because you are not used to doing things like that for self. Think about it. If someone wrapped a gift or cooked dinner for us, we would be so excited and grateful. Providing it for self not only shows your commitment and love to self, but it also decreases the disappointment that comes with solely depending on another person to consistently love us in these ways.

I recommend that you read the *The Five Love Languages* to learn about these concepts in detail, but for now, I will briefly define the five love languages. Read through them and reflect on which two most resonate with you.

1. Words of affirmation. This language uses words to build up the other person. For example, "Thanks for taking out the garbage," not "It's about time you took the garbage out. The flies were going to carry it out for you."
2. Gifts. A gift says, "He/She was thinking about me. Look what he got for me."
3. Acts of Service. This language involves doing something for your spouse that you know he or she would like. Cooking a meal, washing dishes, and vacuuming floors are all acts of service.
4. Quality time. This love language means giving your spouse your undivided attention. That could include taking a walk together or sitting on the couch, talking and listening with the TV off.
5. Physical touch. Holding hands, hugging, kissing, and sexual intercourse are all expressions of this type of love language.[9]

Questions to Identify Your Love Language

Words of Affirmation

1. How do words of affirmation make me feel?
   Love note: Affirmations usher you into a better moment than the one before.

2. When I don't get words of affirmation … (fill in the blank)
   Love note: If words of affirmation are important to you, not receiving them could affect your overall confidence.

Gifts

1. When I receive a gift I know … (fill in the blank)
   Love note: Gifts are amazing to receive, especially when they are well thought-out. However, when people give them just because they think they are supposed to, the gifts have less connected energy.

---

[9] Gary Chapman, "Love Language Profile for Couples," The 5 Love Languages, accessed 2020, https://www.5lovelanguages.com/profile/couples/.

2. How do I feel about giving gifts to me?
   Love note: Gifts can make us feel good, but our feeling good cannot be based on whether or not we receive gifts.

Acts of Service

1. What acts of service make me feel appreciated?
   Love note: It is great to serve others, but one must serve oneself in a healthy way. That way, when you serve others it comes from a healthy place.

2. Do I ever pamper me? For example, do I massage my feet, give myself a manicure, or cook my favorite dinner just for me.
   Love note: It's great when you are treated to these services, but when you do them for yourself, it is self-appreciation, which is the best kind of service.

Quality Time

1. Do I spend quality time with me, or do I always rush my alone time?
   Love note: It's funny how we can give quality time to so many people but when it comes to our own personal time, we rush it.

2. Is it important to me to spend quality time with me daily?
   Love note: Spending time with self births so many deep revelations that only come when you spend time with self.

Physical Touch

1. Do I ever hug myself? Do I ever kiss myself? Do I caress my own hair? If so, how does physical touch from me feel?
   Love note: I have recently started kissing my hand every morning and giving myself a big hug. The feeling has been so intimate for me. Try it!

2. I feel most connected to physical touch because … (fill in the blank)
   Love note: Physical touch has been reported to lower one's blood pressure through a warm touch and releases the "love hormone," oxytocin. Touching is also a key factor to a lasting relationship, due to the intimacy that is felt as a result.

Social Media—Disconnect to Reconnect

Intimacy is best defined as a connection that exists between two people as a result of perceived trust, security, concern, care, and mutually shared goals, beliefs, and values. Intimacy can exist in romantic relationships, sibling relationships, and even among coworkers or military service members who work or fight alongside one another.

The topic of intimacy both excites me and saddens me. My clients have influenced me to accept the title of the intimacy architect. I'm always excited to speak about intimacy and how powerful and essential it is to the success of our relationships. Intimacy connects us more deeply to our truth and exposes our lies as well. You can't be intimate with another if you lack self-intimacy. You have to be aware of your values, self-beliefs, and self-concept; be open to vulnerability; and commit to trusting yourself.

What saddens me is that, because of social media and technology, we have disconnected so far from intimacy. Clients come into my office and break up or, even worse, ask for a divorce over text message. I immediately know that there is a communication issue. It's a little comical when clients are in the same house and they text each other rather than have a conversation because they are so afraid of conflict. Communication is a very important aspect of intimacy. Couples will increase their level of intimacy if they simply spend more time together, talking and discussing issues that are of shared interest or importance and making a point of sharing themselves with each other.

Some of my single clients use social media as a distraction in an effort not to be intimate with self. They have no desire to dig deeper, love themselves more deeply, or be open to vulnerability and transparency at all times. They would rather live a lie, pretending they're someone else on social media. They would rather hide behind likes and their number of followers to determine whether they have a good day or not. If they could only take a step back from social media and create some boundaries so that they can spend more time with themselves. That could consist of placing time limits on social media and only engaging once or twice a day. Another boundary could be not sending long texts or having long discussions over email about subjects that should really be discussed over the phone.

The point I want to make here is that in order to increase intimacy, singles and couples need to turn off the television, the computer, and their cell phones and start having positive self-dialogue or start talking to each other, really talking.

I am not saying that there aren't positives to social media and technology, because there are many upsides, including the ability to connect with people globally with one click. You can do business with potential clients in other countries by sending one message or creating a funnel that requires a couple of links to be registered in your program. Texting makes it easier to check in with your children and monitor their social media accounts. If you like to shop for bargains, you can do that from the privacy of your home. I have met some of the nicest people, who I wouldn't have met had it not been for the connection that the internet provides.

A recent study by Havas Media showed just how much obsessions with social media are affecting the lives and relationships of young millennials and older Generation Z members:[10]

- Almost one-third of those surveyed stated they often exaggerate their statuses and posts on social media, including their relationships.
- Sixty-eight percent state they have used their social networks to check up on ex-partners.
- Seventy-five percent state they believe that social media can ruin or at least harm relationships.

Feeling as though you can't be authentic or being afraid you will be judged for your truth tend to be very good reasons that the statistics above exist. When you don't trust yourself or have not reconciled your past challenges in relationships, you tend to fixate on checking up on your spouse or partner. In addition, social media creates more insecurity, specifically in your relationships with self and others, especially if you are already insecure.

A Cambridge survey asked Americans, "Do you ever feel that you or your family would benefit from having 'technology-free time' where all communications devices are switched off?" About 12 percent said, "All the time," another 12 percent said, "Regularly," and about 36 percent said, "From time to time." That makes a total of 60 percent of respondents who believe unplugging is beneficial.[11]

Tips to Disconnect to Reconnect

Implementing these tips will increase intimacy with self and others and provide you with more quality time to do things that you really love.

---

[10] Bianca London, "Are Mobiles Making Us Obnoxious?," *Daily Mail*, August 20, 2014, https://www.dailymail.co.uk/femail/article-2727999/Are-mobiles-making-obnoxious-Under-25s-likely-inflated-self-esteem-exaggerate-thanks-social-media.html#ixzz5BTI4hZDw.

[11] Liz Soltan, "Digital Responsibility to the Detriment of In-Person Relationships," Digital Responsibility, accessed January 3, 2020, http://www.digitalresponsibility.org/digital-distraction-to-the-detriment-of-in-person-relationships.

- Schedule times for social media and do not engage outside of those times.
- When you are meeting with a friend or your significant other, turn your phone off. Be fully engaged.
- Take a week off of social media.
- Silence your news feed or notifications on social media when you are reconnecting to self or others.
- Start picking up the phone to have meaningful conversations.
- Instead of texting or having rushed phone conversations, consider video chatting. You not only hear the person, but you also see him or her, which means more connecting.

Final Thoughts on Intimacy

In conclusion, "you can't have love without trust. To trust someone means to rely on them. You have confidence in them. You feel safe with them physically and emotionally. Trust is something that two people in a relationship can build together when they decide to do so."[12] If you and a friend or partner can admit your wrongs and speak freely about your feelings, you know you can trust each other. Sharing emotional and financial secrets nurtures trust. If you hide your texts and keep passwords on everything, you could give the impression that you are hiding something. On the other hand, giving your partner permission to answer your phone when it rings indicates you have nothing to hide.

We must trust in order to be trusted. When we trust someone, it keeps our emotions from getting the best of us. Trust comes before love, so if you say you love someone with no trust, it's not love. Love can sometimes cloud judgment, but clarity comes through trust. Trusting yourself first will decrease trust issues with others. When people say, "I don't trust anyone," they are saying they don't trust themselves.

Get Ready to Do Your Work

Tips for Trust

> Trust that you love and accept self for who you are. (*Love note:* It is up to you to do the personal work that will lead you to reach your full potential in trusting someone.)

---

[12] "Trust," Love Is Respect, accessed January 20, 2020, https://www.loveisrespect.org/healthy-relationships/trust/.

➤ Trust that you will not abandon self through conflict, adversity, or speaking your truth.

➤ Trust that you are committed to making your relationship with self a top priority. (*Love note:* By making self your top priority, you will never lose yourself to someone else's needs.)

➤ Trust that you can be sexually and emotionally faithful no matter what the challenge. It's called integrity.

➤ Trust that you will not manipulate, harm, or reject another person if you are not getting your way.

➤ Trust what you know about your relationship to be true instead of allowing other people to speak negatively about who you are.

Exercise 1: Other Ways to Say "I Love You"

Saying "I love you" feels good, but sometimes it loses its power. Sometimes we say "I love myself" but can't even find five things about ourselves that we like. Let's be more intentional about why we love self.

Here are some examples to get you started. These are great statements by themselves, but adding a *because* at the end to explain why you feel that way is even better. This works great if you make these statements to self and to others.

- I appreciate you.
- I adore you.
- You are amazing.
- I respect you.
- You bring me joy.
- I need you.
- I admire you.
- I'm learning from you.
- I am thankful for you.

Exercise 2: Steps for Intimacy with Self

Connecting more deeply to self-intimacy daily is one of the best gifts you can give to self. It has saved me from being depressed many times. My hope is that you will adopt the four intimacies—emotional, intellectual, spiritual, and physical—into your daily life. Use the activities in this exercise to be more intentional about daily self-care.

Emotional

- Reflect in the morning (e.g., daily devotion, meditation, a cozy hot cup of tea). Check in with self midway throughout the day to identify what affected you in a healthy or unhealthy way. Before you go to bed at night, make sure you are at peace or journal your feelings so that you don't go to bed with anger.
- Be mindful with what you're feeling and where you're holding the particular emotion. Don't judge it or try to push it down. Lean into it and allow yourself to feel it. Remember we have to feel to heal.

Intellectual

- Ask yourself what your dreams and visions are. Are they truly yours, or are they influenced by someone else? Are you your own worst critic? If you are, then it's more than likely leading your life. If your critic is negative and an inner liar, then it can determine the outcome of your future.
- Meditate. There are so many ways to meditate, and there is no judgment on which one you choose. If it provides you clarity and peace, then go for it.

Physical

- Look in the mirror. The mirror is an exercise I give my clients. They hate it at first because it's uncomfortable, but once they are comfortable with it, they love it. First, take off your clothes. Second, stand in front of the mirror for five minutes and just let the emotions come. You will walk away with clarity.
- Harness the power of touch. Massage your body. It's great to go to the spa, but there's something special about massaging yourself from head to toe. Who knows best on how to massage you better than you?
- Connect to your breathing. Spend five to ten minutes breathing deeply and pay attention to the quality of your breath. Notice if it's shallow or deep, slow or fast, smooth or jagged, restricted or easy.

Spiritual

- Ask yourself the big questions: What do you believe? What and who do you spiritually connect to? How do you feel when you are the most spiritually connected?
- Write a love letter to self. The love letter is very spiritually connected. Reflect deeply on you and be open to forgiveness and compassion. Pick an age you want to focus on and express all the things you would say presently to yourself at that point in the past. For example, if you are thirty, write a letter to self at twenty-one. Allow your soul to speak. I guarantee you will be healed and comforted.

Reflective Notes

Reflective Notes

Reflective Notes

CHAPTER 8

Till Death Do I Part

First let me say that I realize the traditional wedding vows state, "till death do *us* part," but in this book we are focused on self, so we will use "till death do *I* part." By this I mean commit to *yourself* until the day you die. Whatever may come, never give up on you. Even the best of people can fail you, but God and you will never leave you; it's impossible. You can't run from yourself, so face the challenges, work through them, and get help if you need it as you heal. While working through this process, I have found a friend within myself, and I have often found my own answers to heal any pain. On the other hand, God has also put people in my life to guide me to the answers and the healing that comes from unconditional love.

Layla's Story

Layla was young and ambitious, the definition of a burst of life. Her smile was contagious, and her heart was so giving. She was committed to making others happy and living life to the fullest. She wanted to be a professional singer, although she could have been so many amazing things in life.

The sad realization is that she didn't have everything about herself. All the qualities that people liked, she struggled to accept. She could support everyone else, but when it came to supporting self, she couldn't do that fully. She didn't have the strength to acknowledge some of her fears or pain and ultimately get the help she needed to overcome them. It was much more comfortable to deal with others than to have the courage to save herself.

When things were at their worst, she continued to turn her back on every opportunity to stay committed for better or for worse. If her friends or family were going through their worst, she gave everything of herself. She gave of her reserves until there was nothing left for her.

She thought if she were rich she would be happy. She could buy a big house and a beautiful car and have a fabulous wedding. She thought, *I can take care of everyone.* She never stopped to think about how poor she felt in her soul and how tangible wealth would never be able to pay for the remedy to that. The remedy to feeling poor in one's soul is choosing to be happy every day. It's being able to be happy whether or not you are poor financially. It's staying committed to self for richer or for poorer no matter what. It's painful that she made the choice not to stay on the journey.

She was mentally sick, and no one could see it. What I mean by mentally sick is that she was very depressed. Honestly, most people didn't notice the signs of depression; they just thought she was having a challenging time or season. The fact that she was always smiling gave them a false sense of comfort that everything was okay. Even if someone is smiling and the life of the party, take the time to speak with that person intimately. She was surrounded by individuals who worked in the mental health industry, but perhaps she didn't trust her truth with them, or maybe she didn't know what her truth was. It is no one's fault, but it is a tragedy that so many people missed the opportunity to help her. She lived her life behind the veil. If only she could have been diagnosed with whatever was wrong. If only she could have accepted the option to do what was necessary to get healthy mentally. But once again, she turned her back on self and decided to hide the severe pain she was in.

Love is something she wrote about in her songs, and how beautiful they were. They would truly touch you if you heard them. She gave her all to every performance. People were moved by her enthusiasm and passion. If only she could have given that back to herself. She loved her love interest and sacrificed a lot for him, but again she never provided that for self.

She neglected to commit to every vow, and after years of being in pain and feeling insecure, unseen, and unheard, she decided to break the last vow, which was "till death do I part." She decided to take her own life. Most of those who knew her were in shock, and it was the deepest pain they had ever dealt with. The questions were endless and still are to this day. Some asked how she could be so selfish. But how can someone think about being selfless when he or she has never been selfless, specifically when it comes to his or her own well-being? Another way to think about it is that she was in so much pain and unfortunately saw suicide as the only option. She had a hard time living within herself and her pain. Perhaps she saw death as a way out.

If you are in pain, reach out to me. Along with what I do to help people who are in pain, I also have a network of psychologists and psychiatrists who can help you. If you are contemplating suicide, please call the National Suicide Prevention hotline at 1-800-273-8256.

Self Vows Questions

Dead Relationship

1. Do I sometimes feel dead but physically alive? How will I know if my relationship falls into this category?
    Love note: If you begin to experience unhealthy behavior that kills your spirit, your relationship might be dead.

2. Have I ever felt that my relationship with self began to feel familiar but not in a positive way? What will I do if I'm on that path?
    Love note: Sometimes we can begin to feel that we are mimicking toxic relationships we have witnessed of how others treat themselves.

3. Am I emotionally or physically abusive to myself or others?
    Love note: If your partner calls you names, manipulates you, controls you, hits you, or consistently tears down your self-esteem, you are allowing yourself to be abused.

To Say or Not to Say the Vow

1. How can I take the vows to someone else when I haven't taken the self vows?
    Love note: Most clients want to be married and find the one, but they haven't taken or defined what the vows mean for self.

2. Now that I have taken the vows, did I think about each and every vow before I said it? Did I ask myself if I was prepared to keep them?
    Love note: If you have never made any of the wedding vows to yourself, they may be very difficult to keep with someone else.

Grief

1. Am I a person who leans into my feelings, or do I run from negative emotional experiences, such as the grieving process?

Love note: Grief is one of the hardest emotions and processes to go through. We tend to numb our feelings or just choose to embrace denial or deflection as a way to cope. If your desire is to heal, you have to feel.

2. Do I think crying is weak? If so, how do I deal with hurt, loss, or intense emotions?
Love note: People grieve differently. We should never judge one another for how we go through this process. Crying can be so freeing and a release of negative emotions.

Physical Death

1. Do I have a checklist for when death draws near?
Love note: Having a list of important documents, passwords, and accounts will decrease stress when that time comes.

2. If my partner dies, will I ever open my heart to love again? Or will I choose to stay single?
Love note: Whether or not to marry again is a personal preference. My mom never remarried, and at times I wished she had, both for the companionship and for the experience of emotional intimacy within a partnership. I have witnessed people as old as eighty experience love and partnership again.

As Long As I Shall Live

Another perspective of this vow is welcoming the death of the fake parts of you to make way for the authentic you. It's disconnecting from the parts of us that are dead in order to live. Separating from authenticity breaks the vow of "till death do I part," but the death of the fake self is a commitment to the vow "as long as I shall live." Death of the fake self means burying all things about ourselves that are lies.

Death of the fake self is one of the toughest things I have observed others go through, including myself. It feels like the worst grieving process, and the length of it depends on our resistance. When you have lived with different facets of yourself for years, it's difficult to embrace and execute change. Someone once told me that when you are healthy, you make different choices. The choices you make from an unhealthy place will not be the same choices you make from a place of health. The people you attract from a healthy space will be the opposite of the ones you attract from an unhealthy place. This is especially true when you have to walk away from the self that has kept you in bondage and in fear. It is the most liberating feeling ever when you give yourself permission to speak your truth. Living is breathing air that doesn't feel like it's poisoning your purpose with every breath. Living is synonymous with purpose. Choose to live in this moment.

Grace's Story

"As long as I shall live" is a commitment that I chose to make not only for my kids but for me too. I will continue to breathe in a healthy way so that my kids will have a healthy environment. There was a time in life when there was nothing but darkness in my vision. I had no idea what I wanted in life. I didn't even realize that I was a bit numb. I looked around at my reality; I had an alcoholic family member in my life, an abusive family member, and six siblings. Many times I would pretend that I was asleep just to try to drown out the drama.

I remembered thinking that when I had kids, I would teach them the real meaning of life: love, respect, peace, and truly living your best life!

After I met who I thought was the love of my life, I believed I would have peace and love, but little did I know, I would be heartbroken yet again. The alcoholic family member was my first heartbreak, and now I was experiencing that same heartbreak with the person I thought loved me. It turned out to be a toxic relationship, and because I was unhealthy in some areas myself, I stayed longer than I should have. Life as a whole was getting worse, and I found myself witnessing a murder; someone killed a person in front of me. I was scared and lost, and it was the beginning of the end. After seeing a man lying there, struggling to take his last breath, I asked, *Why me? Why is my life this painful?* Then I realized that I would be raising my first child alone, and I was pregnant with another child.

The yelling and emotional abuse behind closed doors that I witnessed growing up later bled into my own marriage. I was surviving, not living. I realized it wasn't only my spouse who was unhealthy; it was me too. I realized we both had been damaged by our pasts.

The alcohol I hated ended up being my friend to numb the pain. Then the drugs became my friend. Addicted and repeating the pain and bad behaviors of my ancestors, I just wanted to die. I wanted to end it. I realized that what I had seen growing up was reflected in my current behavior and in the behavior I was tolerating from others.

My marriage allowed me to see how much individual work I needed to do. I began to see Dr. Michelle for my marriage and quickly realized that I hadn't taken my self vows, and it was affecting me as a woman, mother, friend, daughter, and wife. I knew I had to make a change. The Self Vows Retreat truly illuminated many things about me and my reactions. I realized how stubborn and resistant I could be out of the fear of change.

As long as I live.

Through all of the pain, hurt, burdens, abandonment, and fear that paralyzed my growth, I started to fight for my freedom.

I attended the Self Vows Retreat and realized what it means to take the vow "as long as I live" to self. The ladies encouraged me in a way that helped me begin to understand the meaning of sisterhood. I realized that change wasn't going to come tomorrow and that the purpose of the retreat was to open my eyes and heart and usher me into change.

I'm still on the road called "work in progress," but I have realized that the meaning of this vow for me is that I can live through anything. I had just been surviving, but living means having joy with every breath. Happiness is a choice.

Exercise for Preparing for Death

Here is a checklist that will help you get your affairs in order in the event of your death. Note: this is not only for elderly people. Death can come at any age, from natural causes or by accident. This may take you some time to do but just get started—step by step.

1. Give someone durable power of attorney to manage your affairs if you become sick and unable to do so yourself.
2. Write a will. "People tend to create a trust."
3. Write an advanced-care directive or living will and give someone medical power of attorney to carry out your wishes about medical treatment at the end of your life.
4. If you have dependent children, name a guardian to take care of them.
5. Ease the trauma of your death for survivors by preplanning your funeral.
6. Provide social security information.
7. Provide information for health insurance, life insurance, homeowner's insurance, car insurance, and long-term care. Include agent names, phone numbers, and policy numbers.
8. Provide a copy of financial power of attorney documents.
9. Provide the location of the original deed for your home.
10. Provide a list of income and assets, including 401(k)s, IRAs, employee pension, veteran benefits, interest, and so on.

11. Provide a list of liabilities, including mortgages, loans, and property taxes. Include what is owed, when payments are due, and contact information.
12. Provide names of banks and account numbers for checking, savings, and credit union.
13. Provide information on investments (property, stocks, bonds) and contact information for your brokers.
14. Provide credit card and debit card names, numbers, and bank contact information.
15. Provide location of a signed, up-to-date will.
16. Provide location of safe-deposit box and key.

Divorcing the Fake Self

There comes a time when you have to leave and bury the fake you. Anything fake isn't real. When you are living a lie, you are in bondage, and deep within, you are longing for freedom! It's hard to leave the things about yourself that have become a part of your daily life, even though they are toxic. We can become content in our pain. I challenge you right now to leave the pain and run to purpose.

Complete the letter template below to introduce your authentic self to your fake self. I'm here with you in spirit, and I know you can do it. I did it, and I have to tell you, I didn't finish my letter in one sitting. It was a process for me to have the courage to truly embrace my truth no matter how scary it was.

Hello, fake self. I need you to pay close attention. We had some good times and some challenging times. However, because of the challenging times, I realized that I needed to release _____ and let in _____. I was so scared of experiencing disappointment because it reminded me of the time when _____, which was painful and made me feel rejected. I'm ready to be _____, _____, and _____ because I just want to be free to be me. I have been so judged, even by myself, but today I'm ready to stop _____ and start _____. I appreciate what you, the fake me, has taught me about me, but it's time for me to face _____ and restructure _____. I'm tired of not using my voice and feeling unheard because I decided to _____ and never _____. I'm ready to tell the truth, not only to me but to _____ and _____. I don't want to continue to live this lie, because it's causing me to _____. I'm ready and willing to love, and you prevent me from doing that freely. I am committed to never faking it again, whatever *it* is. You served a purpose in my life, but our needs and paths are different now. I have no desire to change you, but I do have to commit to changing me. I respect and honor our journey together, but freedom, peace, and love are waiting, and I have to embrace them with my entire being. Hello,_____. I'm so pleased and honored to meet you.

Signed by the authentic me

Reflective Notes

Reflective Notes

Reflective Notes

CHAPTER 9

Taking the Self Vows: I'm All in Forever

Wow. We are here—the final chapter. It's so fitting that a love letter to self is the only thing left to do. However, before I do that, I would love to share an amazing story that, at the time, didn't feel so amazing when I was in the thick of it.

It was August 23, 2019, at ten o'clock at night, and I was searching my computer for my edited manuscript. I was sweating, nervous, and anxious, and then I began to cry uncontrollably. The edited manuscript was not there. My computer had crashed prior, but I knew—or so I thought—that I had saved it, so I wasn't too concerned. I just had faith that it was still there. Well, it wasn't. I felt like I couldn't breathe.

I had written fifteen thousand extra words a month prior to that because of a suggestion from my developmental edit consultant, who encouraged me to flesh out some statements and the love notes. All of was gone. I felt like I was experiencing a death. I felt defeated. I felt like quitting because this wasn't the first time there had been major obstacles with this book. I could hear the vows "for better, for worse," and the more I tried to turn down the volume, the louder it got.

That night, I didn't sleep well at all. I remember leaving a message with a client of mine, letting her know that I would miss my strategy meeting. I was trying not to cry, but she could hear through the last bit of strength that I was hanging on to, the brokenness in my voice and spirit. Funnily enough, she used the vow "for better, for worse" right back at me, prayed for me, and expressed her faith in me. I had no faith in that moment, only nausea. The beautiful soul queen Moya, who wrote the foreword in this beautiful gift, *The Self Vows*, sent me a message that was a summation of "Pause Queen." She told me, "You have the book in your heart, and it will act as the hard drive. So just download it."

I honestly felt as if I couldn't rewrite all that. It was impossible. That part was true. I couldn't rewrite those sections. But little did I know, I would write something new. As I took a walk, had hot lemon water, and took a long bath, I realized that sometimes things have to be washed away to release something new. I realized that I had been emotionally and physically constipated when I first wrote the additions, and now that I had released a lot of that constipation, clarity was present. Of course I owed it to myself and the world to rewrite the story. I guess you know I surrendered, because we are here. I rewrote the sections, and something so beautiful happened: I gained a deeper understanding of self; the self vows; peace, love, and respect for self; and the support that came from the most surprising sources.

Allow me to reintroduce myself. You know the woman who emerged from the above loss. My name is Dr. Michelle R. Hannah, but my friends and loved ones just call me Michelle, Chelle, and B. I call me love because at this point in life, it feels as if that was my name before conception; it just took me a while to grow into it and realize my power. I am the keeper of my beautiful temple (my spirit, my being). I am an evolving mother, daughter, wife, and friend. I speak and teach healing to the brokenhearted and guide them in how to heal emotionally, and I don't let go until the captives are set free.

"The Sovereign LORD has filled me with his Spirit. He has chosen me and sent me to bring good news to the poor, to heal the broken-hearted, to announce release to captives and freedom to those in prison" (Isa. 61:1). That scripture was given to me when I was in grade school, and I am convinced that is why I have remained relentless, because deep within my self belief, I was connected to this scripture. I walk in any space, and I shift the entire frequency that makes you want to evolve, do better, and live authentically.

Now I can write this love letter. Enjoy!

The Love Letter to Self

Michelle, to have and to hold from this day forward, I take you. Everything about you I have. No matter what you go through, no matter the quirks, no matter the imperfections, I have you. I hold you up no matter what, and if you're down, I'm committing to hold you and support you through your pain and sadness.

Michelle, you are going to move forward daily and not regret or resent the past. You can depend on me to be there when the past attempts to consume you with guilt or shame. I will carry you over every mountain and through every storm.

Michelle, you have had to go through the worst to get to the better, but you have learned so many lessons. You have learned to be truthful no matter what. You have learned to stay committed no matter the situation. You are committed for better or for worse.

Michelle, you have lost a lot, both tangible and intangible. You have also gained a lot, both intangible and tangible. I am so proud that you have let go of the poverty state of mind and committed to a prosperous state of mind. You are no longer thinking about things that are not productive. Remember you have the motivation to make money and create generational wealth, but more than anything, you are wealthy in spirit. For richer, for poorer, you can come through anything. Trust your quantitative and qualitative self.

Michelle, you have been through a plethora of illnesses. The pain, the tears, the embarrassments, and the sacrifice have all built character. I know that you have felt like you were a hostage in your own body, but know that you are free every time you overcome obstacles and get out of bed, regardless if your pain is peaking at a ten. In sickness and in health, keep pushing no matter what.

Michelle, I am so proud of you that you have learned to cherish your life. At one point you didn't. Keep fighting and keep up the treatment, and you will be able to have a high quality of life. Just keep believing. Michelle, love yourself with everything you have. To love and to cherish means to love self unconditionally, and that will keep you on the path to keeping this vow.

Michelle, remember the times you were in so much pain that you contemplated ending it all so the pain would stop? The beauty is that you realized your worth and began to value your life. To death do I part no matter what comes. The day will come when it's your time to leave this earth, and that's the only way that you will transition. Until then, fight on!

Michelle, live your best life. Don't go back and forth with people who don't know you or love you. Live how you want to live, and do what makes you feel free and happy. As long as you shall live means to live beyond the pain and fear.

Thank you for sharing this space with me and taking the journey to truly reflect on self. I challenge you to write your own love letter. Peace and blessings!

In Closing

Now that you have written your love letter to self and completed this book, you are ready to live, not just survive. These seven vows have changed your perspective and how you reflect, deepened your intimacy, provided tools and tips on navigating through the self vows, and ushered you into living your authentic life.

Life is not easy, and it's not supposed to be. Think about life as a classroom, and we will be in it until we take our last breath. We are here to teach and be students; both will prove beneficial to our legacies. The exercises in this book are not just one-time assignments; they are for the rest of your journey. I will never stop scripting, educating myself on finances, writing love letters to myself, reading tips on positive self-talk, keeping an eye out for stress triggers, exploring communication tools, checking in on my mental and physical health, or desiring to live as long as I have breath. I want the same for you, so know that implementing these items in your daily life will manifest your dreams and create a healthy lifestyle.

You have everything you need inside of you. All the answers are there. It's absolutely helpful to take advice. However, your truth and what's best for you is always found within. You are responsible for your life. If you are waiting for someone to save you, then stop wasting your time. How about you rescue yourself? Remember to accept what is, forgive the past, and move forward. Listen to self and don't get off track with distractions that don't serve you. If you are numb to your feelings and disconnected from your truth, then it will be very difficult to hear your inner truth. You can't give what you don't have. Therefore, keep your cup full and overflowing. My cup is overflowing with love, gratitude, self-care, and self love. Know that you are loved, and no matter what you've been through, love is always there, waiting to hold you, heal you, encourage you, save you, and love you past any fear or pain.

What is God's dream for you? Focus on whatever that is in this moment and what you need to do in the next moment to keep moving forward toward your dream. The biggest choices begin and end with you. Until you let go of what's behind you, you will not be able to embrace what's in front of you. If you're scared, I give you permission to let go and let God restore, rejuvenate, and reconnect you back to self.

I love you, and I believe in you. I'm a phone call or an email away, and I would love to hear about all the amazing twists and turns of your journey. Trust me, there will be some twists, but enjoy the process no matter how challenging it is. Wake up every morning and commit to your self vows, and contact us for the next Self Vows Retreat so that you can come and experience the entire weekend. I know this book has resonated with you and your heart is open to receive something new and transforming. I realize that you need some guidance, and that is what our programs are here to do—emotionally heal yourself, connect yourself more deeply to intimacy, and help yourself live authentically. Stop and don't do another thing until you reach out to me so that we can further evolve what you have learned through this book. You can follow me and contact me through these channels:

- Instagram: michelle_r_hannah
- Facebook: Mikel Life Coaching
- Website: michellerhannah.com
- Email: info@michellerhannah.com

Be happy and healthy, and I love you with all that overflows within.

Reflective Notes

Reflective Notes

Reflective Notes

ABOUT THE AUTHOR

Dr. Michelle R. Hannah, through her life's medical challenges, overwhelming love for humanity, her concern for people's health and emotional well-being, and her commitment to living authentically, is among the most influential women today. Michelle's family, education, and personality have molded her for life as a resounding voice for the brokenhearted and those who desire to be free.

In 2004, Michelle moved from California to Washington, DC, and founded the Celebrate Life Foundation. The foundation is dedicated to educating people about HPV, which causes cervical and other cancers. Through its many programs, including Stomp Out Cancer (designed for sororities and fraternities), Teens Against HPV, and the one and only Survivors Pageant, lives are being saved. Elevation brings change, and although Michelle made the tough decision to close the foundation's doors six years ago, she is still dedicated to providing education and awareness about HPV and its relationship to cervical cancer.

Michelle has held several leadership positions, including assistant dean of admissions and manager of strategic partnerships. Currently, she is a master relationship coach, author, public speaker, and entrepreneur. She is the proud mother of a college graduate who is smart, strong-willed, beautiful, and talented.

Michelle's remarkable spirit, determination, motivation, and personal experiences are the building blocks of her respect for human dignity and social change. Born and raised in Southern California, she received her undergraduate degree in psychology, an MBA, and a master's degree in teaching and learning with technology. Recently she earned doctorate in spiritual counseling.

Michelle has coached marriage and family counselors on creating a deeper connection with their clients and how to write more engaging curriculum for their workshops, seminars, and group sessions. She has worked with support group facilitators on how to organize their sessions. She is respected in her industry and is an accomplished author of *The Breaking Point: A Full-Circle Journey* and workbook. Her second book, *The Vows:*

A Workbook for Marriage Success and Understanding Yourself, is ushering couples and people desiring to be married into a deeper intimacy connection, emotional healing, and authentic living. Michelle has helped more than five hundred couples stay together and embrace evolution daily.

Michelle is a dynamic and electrifying speaker. Her public speaking career spans over fifteen years, and audiences everywhere report feeling as though they are in a personal conversation with Michelle because of her engaging and interactive approach. It's always a challenge for her to leave because people want to have a session directly after.

BIBLIOGRAPHY

Chapman, Gary. "Love Language Profile for Couples." The 5 Love Languages. Accessed 2020. https://www.5lovelanguages.com/profile/couples/.

"Emotions and Feelings." Heart and Stroke Foundation. Accessed 2019. https://www.heartandstroke.ca/heart/recovery-and-support/emotions-and-feelings.

Harvey, Don. *The Spiritually Intimate Marriage.* Kentwood, MI: Baker Books, 1991.

"Trust." Love Is Respect. Accessed January 20, 2020. https://www.loveisrespect.org/healthy-relationships/trust/.

Joseph, Stephen. "7 Qualities of Truly Authentic People." *What Doesn't Kill Us* (blog). *Psychology Today,* August 29, 2016. https://www.psychologytoday.com/us/blog/what-doesnt-kill-us/201608/7-qualities-truly-authentic-people.

Kaufman, Scott Barry. "Narcissism and Self-Esteem Are Very Different." *Beautiful Minds* (blog). *Scientific American.* October 29, 2017. https://blogs.scientificamerican.com/beautiful-minds/narcissism-and-self-esteem-are-very-different/.

L., Coleen. "Emotional Intimacy." https://www.selfgrowth.com/articles/ColeenL1.html.

London, Bianca. "Are Mobiles Making Us Obnoxious?" *Daily Mail,* August 20, 2014. https://www.dailymail.co.uk/femail/article-2727999/Are-mobiles-making-obnoxious-Under-25s-likely-inflated-self-esteem-exaggerate-thanks-social-media.html#ixzz5BTI4hZDw.

Pillay, Srini. "Managing Our Emotions Can Save Your Heart." *Harvard Health Blog.* May 9, 2016. https://www.health.harvard.edu/blog/managing-emotions-can-save-heart-201605099541.

Soltan, Liz. "Digital Responsibility to the Detriment of In-Person Relationships." Digital Responsibility. Accessed January 3, 2020. http://www.digitalresponsibility.org/digital-distraction-to-the-detriment-of-in-person-relationships.

Printed in the United States
By Bookmasters